# INDIE AUTHOR MAGAZINE

I0096461

# HELLO AND WELCOME!

I'm Indie Annie, and I'm thrilled you're reading this gorgeous full-color version of IAM. Did you know that you can also access all the information, education, and inspiration in our app? It's available on both the iOS App Store and Google Play. And for those that prefer to listen to me read articles, you can pop over to Spotify or our website. Happy Reading!

*X*

IndieAuthorMagazine.com

# first draft styles

## 26

### BATTLING THE FIRST DRAFT AND WINNING

Strategies for finishing when you think you can't.

## 33

### TACKLING THE FIRST DRAFT ONE DAY AT A TIME

Small habits of consistency can mean big results over time.

## 38

### DICTATING YOUR WAY TO A FIRST DRAFT

Tell yourself a story and finish in no time!

## 48

### SCRIVENER

Breaking down the new features in Windows and new hacks for everyone.

## ON THE COVER

## REGULAR COLUMNS

## THE WRITE LIFE

## TYPEWRITER TALES

# INDIE AUTHOR MAGAZINE

**PUBLISHER**
Chelle Honiker

**MANAGING EDITORS**
Erika Everest
Robyn Sarty

**REGULAR CONTRIBUTORS**
Patricia Carr
Ashli Faron
Fatima Fayez
Kasia Lasinska
Merri Maywether
Lasairiona McMaster

**CREATIVE DIRECTOR**
Alice Briggs

**STAFF WRITERS**
Sìne Màiri MacDougall
Elaine Bateman
Laurel Decher
Chrishaun Keller Hanna
Marion Hermannsen
Anne Lown
Susan Odev

**CONTRIBUTORS**
Kevin McLaughlin

**PUBLISHER**
Athenia Creative
6820 Apus Dr.
Sparks, NV, 89436 USA
775.298.1925

# From the Publisher

Done is better than perfect. Just finish the thing. You can't edit a blank page.

All great advice for writers when they're in the middle of the first draft slog. *Keep going.*

But what happens when the words literally won't come? When the muse won't show up?

Common advice for when you've got writer's block (which my friend Jackie Dana has always maintained does not exist) is to write something outrageous to break up the monotony and get your juices flowing. Kill a character. Someone start a fight. Have them do something opposite to what they would normally do.

Make them all vampires.

That last tip is mine. I know from personal experience and three wins for NaNoWriMo (National Novel Writing Month) that it is an effective strategy to finish … a terrible first draft. Anne Lamott affectionately calls them "shitty first drafts", which I much prefer. Everyone's first draft is awful—and it should be. It's the first time you're telling yourself the story. There's no nuance or snappy dialog. It's just you herding kittens to get the worst version of the thing somewhere you can hate it and then move on to making it something you hate less.

From the publishing and marketing perspectives, you'll start with shitty first drafts too.

You'll upload the wrong cover to KDP. Your Facebook ads will be expensive and you won't know if you're selling books because of them. Your website will be ugly.

You'll decide to quit 457,878,227 times a month, if you're like most of us. Keep going.

Every mistake is a lesson. An iteration. A chance to pivot.

You'll get better. You will. There's science that proves it, but you can just trust me on this. If you keep going and learn from every experiment, whether it's writing better dialog, or finding better keywords, or creating a checklist that keeps track of the right cover to upload, you'll start to see success.

This month's issue is all about these first drafts and how to finish. You'll find a wealth of tried and true tips and resources to help you, and I highly recommend these strategies over my NaNoWriMo one. Unless you write vampires.

Keep Going,
Chelle
Publisher
*Indie Author Magazine*

# From the Creative Director

In this issue, we're continuing to follow the basic process of creating a book. Outlining last time, First Drafts this. It seems like a fairly straight-forward topic. However, our writers and editors have crafted some fascinating articles we expect will provide you with some new strategies to incorporate into your drafting workflow.

Planning to use poisonous plants in your mystery? Be sure and give the Devil in the Details a read—we might even add to your TBR pile! In the Mindset article, we'll help you get through the muddy middle, something that's claimed several of my projects! And, our Op-Ed this month is all about Vella, Amazon's foray into serialization.

Whether you write serials or epically long fantasy tomes, we hope you find good encouragement at the pace of your drafting and production schedule with our interview of Jami Albright and the feature on taking it one day at a time.

As always, we expect you'll discover more than you expected and at least a couple actionable ideas to inspire your own author career, wherever that leads.

Onward and Upward!

Alice Briggs
Creative Director,
*Indie Author Magazine*

# From the Managing Editor

After the excitement of Outlining, that first glimmer of the idea that's going to be the most amazing story ever, we come to First Drafts. It's time to roll up our sleeves and do the hard work.

One of the hardest parts of writing a novel is finding time to write. Time is our most precious commodity and there are so many demands on it. It's easy to get overwhelmed and feel "I just don't have time for writing; it doesn't fit in my life now." This is doubly true for newer authors, when you don't have an established fan base waiting for your book. You may get the sense that there's no point, that you're just wasting time.

In this issue, we'll help you get through that first draft, by finding ways to find time. Start small to build daily habits that will set the foundation for a long term career. Make the most of those breaks that you have, that you may not even recognize as possible writing time. Discover the joy of dictation—once you get past the awkwardness, it can be a great way to squeeze more time out of your day, and more words out of your time. We also look at collaboration as a path to achieving more through working with others.

Wherever you are in your manuscript, and in your writing journey, I hope you find some thoughts to inspire you within these pages.

Happy reading and happy writing,

Erika Everest
Managing Editor
*Indie Author Magazine*

# From the Managing Editor

Before I get to this month's topic, I want to say thank you to everyone who has supported us in our launch. Seeing how the indie author community embraced the magazine reassures us that this is something we need. So thank you to each of you who came to our launch party, bought a subscription, or even shared on social.

This month, as we move through the life of a book, our theme is first drafts, and it is my hope that the information these articles contain will help you write your best book yet. First drafts can be the hardest part of novel writing. Whether it's the accusatory blinking of the cursor on the blank page or the murky middle slowing you down, the task of writing 70,000 words or more can seem insurmountable.

But first drafts don't have to be—they can be the stage upon which your story shines. To me, first drafts are the playhouse of the imagination, where anything can happen and there are no limits.

Even if you're following an outline, there is room for creative freedom. Let the characters run free. Let the story flow from within you. Because that is how we write stories that are true. True to you, and true to the characters.

But books aren't all magic and play. They take hard work and focus. Whether it's developing a daily writing habit or amping up your dictation skills, I hope we can help you level up your writing.

Because the world needs your book.

Robyn Sarty
Managing Editor,
*Indie Author Magazine*

# Vella: KDP Gets Serialous

On April 13th, Amazon's Kindle Direct Publishing (KDP) announced a new program: Kindle Vella, a home for serial stories. Like Kindle Unlimited and Kindle Worlds before it, indie authors around the world have shown enormous interest in the upcoming program, which is due to launch this summer. But like all Amazon programs, we authors are left to wonder: is this another KU or another Kindle Worlds? One of those programs worked extremely well, but the other left a lot of authors reeling when it shut down.

Today we will look at the Kindle Vella program, examine it in detail, and attempt to determine if this is worth our time—or if we'd be better off writing something else.

## WHAT'S A SERIAL?

Serials are long stories told in small slices called episodes. Authors publish them on serial platforms like Radish, Royal Road, and Tapas, uploading new episodes on a regular basis for their readers. It's a lot like many broadcast TV shows; readers show up for the next installment of the ongoing story.

While episode length varies a bit from one serial site to another, Vella is allowing uploads of episodes from 600 to 5000 words in length. This gives the writer plenty of space to work with for each episode, but episodes are not always the same thing as chapters in a novel (although they can be similar).

Where a novel might have a "slow point" that spans an entire chapter, with a serial there is a longer break between each episode. With this format, it's even more important to create story hooks that keep the reader entertained and wanting desperately to know what happens next. If you allow the reader to feel like they've reached a satisfying conclusion for even a single episode, they may jump to another story.

## WHAT ABOUT VELLA?

Kindle Vella is Amazon's upcoming entry. They announced it will launch on iOS devices and web browsers only, and will only be available to US authors at launch. However, they've also said they plan to launch an Android app and expand author access to other countries.

To access Vella, go to the KDP help pages, click the link to Kindle Vella on the left side bar, and then go from there to the section about uploading episodes. It'll take you to a special Vella interface.

We can already upload as many episodes as we'd like. It's a simple matter to create a new Serial (that's the overall story) and then upload several initial Episodes for that serial. Most writers with serial experience are suggesting authors launch with 5-6 episodes. The first three episodes will be a "free sample" for the reader, so you want something after those first three. But we don't want to upload dozens of episodes right away, generally speaking. Part of the fun for these readers is to explore content as it is uploaded.

## VELLA DOWNSIDES

The big one is the exclusivity clause—but bear with me, because it isn't as bad as that sounds. There's a great deal of confusion over what Vella exclusivity means.

KDP is requiring the following:

- No Vella work can previously have been published as a "long-form work" (like a novel). So we cannot split up existing books for this program.
- Likewise, before we publish any episodes of a serial as part of a long-form book (like, compile the episodes into a novel), *all* episodes of that serial must be taken down from Vella.
- Episodes *can* be uploaded on other sites, too. But they must be in episode format and must not be freely available on the web.

Obviously this makes things a little trickier for folks who usually write novels. We *can* put our episodes up on other serial sites. We can also release them to fans on our websites or Patreon, provided they're behind a paywall. But we have to take the serial down from Vella before compiling it into a "regular" book. This of course means delaying the income we'll make from sales of those books.

Another possible downside involves author royalties. At present, readers will pay for tokens which they use to buy episodes at a rate of one token per hundred words (a 1000 word episode costs ten tokens; a 1099 episode is also ten tokens; a 1101 word episode is eleven tokens). It looks like the author income sits at about three times what KU pays per thousand words, but that number is *definitely* still in flux, as we won't know how Amazon plans to discount or give away free tokens until after the program goes live. I expect that number to drop. How much? We don't know.

> " Create story hooks which will keep the reader entertained and wanting desperately to know what happens next. "

Those are some hefty downsides. We have to choose between publishing as a Vella/serial work or a long-form novel, and like KU we're not sure what the pay scale looks like (although initial indications look good).

However, Vella might well be worth it. As we saw when KU started, early adopters of new KDP programs often have a strong advantage over later arrivals. I'd expect the same here. We don't know how well readers will take to this new platform, but serials are popular, so it's likely to work if Amazon pushes hard.

The most important element for me is that we can always take the works down. If Vella flops, I can immediately take any serials I've uploaded down from Vella and compile them into novels. The only downside is I have to delay the full-book upload. For me, the chance to get in on the ground floor of something new outweighs the small delay. I'm planning on launching several serials in Vella when it goes live. Those which do well there will get continued. Those which don't will get taken down and compiled into novels.

I see two approaches likely to succeed in this program. The first is going "all in" on serials: setting up one or more Vella serials and also putting those episodes live on as many other paid serial sites as possible. The second would be an "iron in the fire" approach, where the author puts a serial in Vella to test it out but remains *primarily* focused on regular novels. I believe either option has a good shot at working out well regardless how successful Vella ends up being.

> "For me, the chance to get in on the ground floor of something new outweighs the small delay.

## Kevin McLaughlin

Kevin McLaughlin is the USA Today bestselling author of 83 books. He writes mostly science fiction and fantasy, and is also the author of The Coffee Break Novelist and You Must Write. He's enjoyed reading and writing serials for decades.

# IAM OPINIONATED

Last month,
we asked our readers:
**Kindle Vella: Future of
Publishing or Just a Fad?**

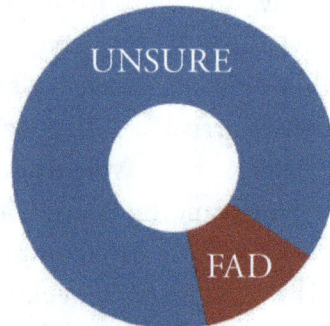

UNSURE

FAD

87.5% of responders are
unsure if Vella is the future of
publishing or just a fad. 12.5%
of responders feel it's just a fad.

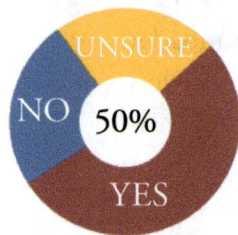

UNSURE

NO 50% 

YES

**Will you publish
via Vella?**

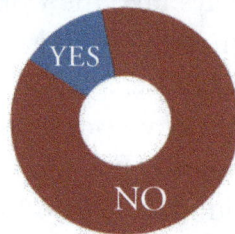

YES

50%

NO

**Do you currently
publish serials?**

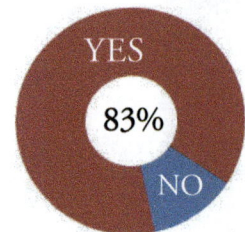

YES

83%

NO

**Those considering Vella who will
be publishing serials for the first
time**

I'm jumping in just
in case it takes off.
I missed the gold
rush of KU2.0.

**Shannon**

It is evolution of
the market and
sounds like it
will suit people
who want short
sharp content on a
regular basis.

**Steve**

I want to keep my
options open as
Amazon has such a
huge reach.

**Jamie**

I'm not sure Vella's
a fad or the future,
just a different way
to consume litera-
ture. And probably
one that will find
its niche audience
and thrive.

**Josh**

My daughter has been reading episodic, or short standalone stories, online for as long as I can remember. Whether it's Creepy Pastas or an app she had where stories were told in the form of text messages. For her generation it's a natural evolution of the way they already consume short or episodic tales. But reading serials is also a very old idea. People always mention Dickens and Arthur Conan Doyle when they talk about Vella. I think it is neither a fad or the future of publishing. I think it has always been a part of reading in some form and always will be.

**Andrew**

While it's something that's intriguing, and there is definitely a place for serialised storytelling in this way, I'm going to be concentrating on my long form novel writing for the foreseeable future. I'll be very interested to see how Vella plays out though.

**G.M.**

Given industry clout, I imagine Amazon could make it a worthy venture if they have the will.

**Tom**

# THIS MONTH'S QUESTION:

## AUTHORS ON SOCIAL

Is social media a good way to connect or a waste of time?

Have your say!
Vote here
https://writelink.to/iamopinionated

# Dear Indie Annie,

*I love my characters. I love seeing them live out their lives, and making wonderful things happen to them. But my critique partner says my story is boring as nothing bad ever happens. How can I make my story more interesting without being mean to my characters?*
*Help!*
*Nice in Newcastle*

## DEAR NICE,

Thank you so much for your letter. It is a wonderful thing to be the creator of new worlds, new lives, isn't it? Planting the seed and watching it grow. We are the gods of our little universes. We nurture and care for our creations and want them to thrive.

Our readers want that too. They want to see your characters grow. They need to be taken along on their journeys, their adventures, their quests. In real life, people grow through facing challenges and overcoming obstacles. As the gods of our characters' world, we need to be cruel to be kind. We all have drama in our lives. We all face times of conflict, loss and grief. It is part of the human condition and without it, your characters will not feel authentic and your story will be flat and uninteresting.

To quote Whitney Houston in the Olympic anthem: One moment in time to "taste the sweet" we must "face the pain." If your characters only experience the best that life offers, will it not lose its magic? Realising a goal after you have worked hard to achieve it has more value than being handed it on a plate with no effort.

From your god-like position, you can give your characters opportunities to develop and grow, even to thrive. By providing them with a series of obstacles to overcome, their eventual victory will be all the sweeter. Through creating conflicts between them, even over small things like the choice of breakfast cereal, or larger more political, socio-economic or cultural

Need help from your favorite Indie Aunt?
Ask Dear Indie Annie a question at
IndieAnnie@indieauthormagazine.com

differences, you are offering your characters a chance to change their worldview, to try new things, to embark on fresh adventures. Providing your characters with challenges to overcome, they will discover hidden strengths and talents.

Think of a sword. A beautifully crafted sword is beaten, heated, and plunged in icy water repeatedly. The master sword maker knows that this is the only way to create a weapon able to withstand the full force of battle. It is the process of heating, beating, and cooling that forges both the strength and the beauty of the finished piece.

You don't say what genre you write in, but all stories require conflict and drama to keep the reader engaged. There may not be any epic battles in sweet romance, but there are misunderstandings and missed opportunities that drive the narrative to the happily ever after.

All stories require an inciting incident when the main character's life changes. Every story has a climax, that moment when everything before comes to a dramatic head. And a resolution. This story structure is as old as time and works because this is the adventure we as readers, or listeners (via audiobooks, as in days of old), crave. People need to be engaged with your character's journey to keep turning the page, and conflict creates that need to read on.

You don't have to be super mean. Conflict can be as trivial as a misunderstanding about the time the train leaves and missing your connection. Or can be as huge as finding out you have inherited magical powers or that Darth Vader is your father.

Your characters may hate you at the time, but in the end, when they emerge triumphant, they will thank you and so will your readers.

Happy writing,
Indie Annie X

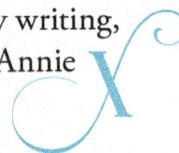

# 10 TIPS FOR CLUBHOUSE

Clubhouse is the latest social media platform. It's an audio-only platform where people engage in conversation in groups called "rooms." Some rooms invite everyone to participate, whereas in others you're only a listener. You can select your interests to help Clubhouse identify the content you want to see in your Hallway (the main page), but you can also shape what rooms you see by following people and clubs that interest you.

## 1 ADD A PROFILE PHOTO

Your name and profile photo may be the only thing people see on Clubhouse, especially if they first see you in a room. Choose an attractive photo that is well-lit and represents who you are. You can change your photo regularly; however, it may become confusing to people who aren't familiar with you. Wait to switch your photo until you become a regular member and people get to know you.

Pro-tip: Use a photo app to tweak your background to make it easier for people to find you when you're talking in a crowded room. "This is [Your Name] speaking; I'm the one with the orange background."

Pro-tip: Some people use props in their photos to display what they do. For example, authors upload photos of them holding or signing their latest books.

## 2 CRAFT A COMPELLING BIO

Use the bio section to pitch yourself to people scrolling across your profile. What is it that you want to be known for? The first line of your bio is sometimes the only thing people see when they click on your profile photo. People rarely click to "see more," so make that first line the most compelling part about you.

Pro-tip: Use plenty of emojis to draw people's attention and showcase a sense of humor. The more creative you can be with the use of emojis, the more playful you will appear.

Pro-tip: Link your Instagram and Twitter accounts so that people can follow you on other platforms and you can grow your social media following.

## ③ LEARN THE ETIQUETTE

When you join a room, you start "in the audience" (listening only.) There's a hand icon in the lower right corner of your screen. Click on it to "raise your hand" and let the moderators know that you want to share in the discussion. Don't get offended if you're not raised to "the stage" (invited to be a speaker.) Be patient. It could be that they don't have time to take questions or that they're not looking at their screen.

It can be easy for people to talk over one another in Clubhouse. When you're invited to join the speakers, immediately mute your mic. Only unmute it when you're ready to speak.

Pro-tip: To avoid speaking over someone, pay attention to the microphone icon on the screen and see if the talker mutes themselves.

Introduce yourself when you first talk, stay on topic, keep your participation to under thirty seconds to avoid monopolizing the conversation, and indicate you're done talking by saying "done."

If you've had enough of a room, click the button that says Leave Quietly. There's no need to announce your departure; this isn't an airport.

Pro-tip: If you see flashing microphones, don't worry. This indicates agreement or clapping, an endorsement of what the speaker is saying.

## ④ FOLLOW PEOPLE AND JOIN CLUBS

In order for Clubhouse to show you live rooms that you would be interested in, you need to follow people and join clubs. The more people you follow, the more rooms it will show you. You'll be able to join them and listen or participate.

At the bottom of every bio are icons for the clubs that person is a member of. Browse them and see if you'd like to follow the same clubs.

You can see what upcoming talks are happening in the club by swiping on their page. You can add the events to your calendar or ask for a Clubhouse reminder when the talk is happening.

Not finding a club that holds your interest? Start your own!

Pro-tip: If you see rooms in your Hallway you'd rather not show up again, swipe them from left to right and they should disappear from your Hallway.

## ⑤ START A ROOM

The best way to get used to the Clubhouse platform is to start a room. Clubhouse has several options to choose from: a Locked room where you choose who can join, a Social room where people you follow can see it in the Hallway and pop in, and an Open room that will appear to everyone in Clubhouse.

Get accustomed to the different levels of privacy afforded to you in Clubhouse by testing a room of every type.

Take it a step further and add a topic to your room and try to keep guests on topic. That helps you see how to moderate a room, and to understand the work it takes to make sure the environment remains fun and welcoming.

Pro-tip: Starting a room consistently, either at the same time or same day, can help you create a circle of regular attendees. You'll notice some familiar faces popping in to chat and it's a great opportunity to network and connect with others.

## 6 BE PRODUCTIVE BY JOINING WRITING SPRINTS

Clubhouse can be a time suck at the beginning as you get used to this new social media app. It's easy to enter rooms and lose track of time. That's why we recommend joining rooms focused on increasing productivity. They will ensure you get words. You can be on Clubhouse and writing!

There are several sprinting clubs where you can join other authors for writing sprints. It's a great way to ensure you're being productive while networking with like-minded individuals.

Pro-tip: Join Author Arena Writing club for regular sprint rooms.

## 7 ADJUST YOUR NOTIFICATIONS

Click on Settings (the gear symbol in the upper right corner of your profile) and change the Frequency from Very Frequent to Very Infrequent. As discussed above, Clubhouse can eat up a lot of your time especially if you get a case of FOMO (Fear Of Missing Out). Adjusting your notifications can help eliminate that temptation a little.

On the other hand, if there's someone you absolutely can't miss, click the alarm bell icon on their bio and you'll be notified when they're talking in a room.

## 8 JOIN THE CLUBHOUSE TOWN HALL EVERY SUNDAY

Clubhouse is continuously rolling out updates and improvements. The founders have regular Sunday meetings explaining all their rollouts. If you can't make the Clubhouse Town Hall meeting, you can click on Settings and select What's New to go to the Release Notes page.

Pro-tip: Be sure to continuously upgrade the app so that you don't miss on the latest developments.

## 9 JOIN CLUBHOUSE AUTHORS FACEBOOK GROUP

To find out about when more rooms are happening and get access to resources from talks, join the Clubhouse Authors Facebook group. Started by Monica Leonelle, the Facebook group has turned into a tremendous resource for authors to circulate information widely. We're still waiting for Clubhouse to provide a direct messaging option. Until then, Clubhouse Authors will keep you informed about what rooms are scheduled during the week.

https://www.facebook.com/groups/clubhouseauthors

## 10 HAVE FUN!

The purpose of Clubhouse is to connect with people. There are thousands of rooms happening every single day. Have fun and experiment by joining different ones. Be social and speak up in rooms. Clubhouse is designed for lurkers to stay silent and listen, but you're missing out if you don't speak up and connect with other people. Join author communities and attend the rooms with topics you're interested in. Writing can be a solitary career, but with Clubhouse it doesn't need to be. ◼

Fatima Fayez

# First Drafts

## Find the Below Words on First Drafts in the Puzzle

```
M I N I M U M V I A B L E P R O D U C T
Y H A B I T N Y J R Y Z N Z Y W H M D N
C O L L A B O R A T I O N J R S Y Y M Y
N M F E Y R K L I W I D M I I L D J D Y
E U I Q C P D V K T Y M T N I E Q Z W J
T S R W D I I D C J D I I A L M B N W M
S E S X J T T E N I N F D D L E X Q N D
I R T G A Y F C C G V Y D Q G D O N E P
S X D E Y R R T A T D I P A P J Y T X W
N Y R K E Y A Y M R M K P H G U O R B Q
O C A P B T F M D Y P K H E I N L E I N
C G F L I I D R D N N W Y G P R D N L W
V T T O M N G D M A E R D K M Q D Y Q M
Y N N A J T U N L M R E L K V B T Q D Z
N Y G M T M M B T W X R H R Q Q L L L T
M L N G Q Q X Y R Z Q Y Y T D Y N W L N
```

| | |
|---|---|
| Blank Page | Habit |
| Collaboration | Heinlein |
| Consistency | Minimum Viable Product |
| Creativity | Muse |
| Daily | Muddy Middle |
| Dictation | Perfection |
| Done | Practice |
| Finish | Rough |
| First Draft | The End |
| Gamify | Writing |

# Blood, Sweat, & Tears

We've all heard the expression "blood, sweat, and tears." *I've put my blood, sweat, and tears into this project.* This month we will meet an author who did exactly that.

Let me introduce Jami Albright. Every week, authors around the world can catch an hour with Jami on her podcast, "Wish I'd Known Then." Jami, her co-host Sarah Rosett, and their guests discuss their chosen paths that led them to success in the indie author business.

Jami and I first met in 2017 at the Smarter Artist Summit. Over lunch, authors new to the indie writing scene discussed what we had done to arrive at our varying levels of success. Jami's story would be the one that stuck with all of us.

She had just launched her first book, *Running from a Rock Star*, which was resting nicely at the top of the Amazon charts. Jami freely shared that this was a bootstrap project. What she lacked in money, she made up for with heart and soul.

That romantic comedy is still in the top 5,000 in the Amazon store four years later.

Fast forward to April 2021. Jami and I had a chance to catch up via a zoom chat. We revisited that conversation from four years ago. This time I asked deeper questions about the story that stuck, and the subsequent ones, and her approach to the writing process.

## HER STORY BEGINS WITH A STORY

Moving is hard on a family. Routines change, friends are far away, and rebuilding takes time. When Jami's family moved from Austin to Houston, TX, she started reading romance to fill in the gaps created by the transition. Her foray into a new genre began with *Twilight*, which Jami affectionately called "my gateway drug to romance." From there, she read other romance novels.

Some would call what happened next fate; others, a sign. Her friend recommended *Sugar Daddy* by Lisa Kleypas. This was before Kindle e-readers were popular, so Jami was hesitant to buy the book. The opportunity to purchase the book her friend recommended came in the least likely of circumstances.

"Walgreens had the hardback on sale for five dollars. And, I thought, well, it's right next to the register. I could just get it and get out." Jami left the store with her new purchase. That book led to making another friend in Barnes and Noble. Jami shared her new find, *Sugar Daddy*. That friend recommended Susan Elizabeth Phillips', *Nobody's Baby But Mine*.

The newest read was so funny; Jami laughed through tears. It was the first time she had laughed that hard since her move to Houston. "I remember thinking if I can make somebody feel this way, that would be the best thing in the whole world. But even then, I still hadn't considered writing."

> This was a bootstrap project. What she lacked in money, she made up for with heart and soul.

# Jami Albright

This experience with a well-written novel would be the impetus for the blood, sweat, and tears story. Years later, as a birthday present for the friend she met in Barnes and Noble, Jami started a novel. She wrote herself into a corner and didn't finish the story. Still, she shared what she had tried with her friend. Her friend laughed in all the right places and encouraged Jami to continue with the story. They brainstormed ideas for a story that Jami titled *Rock My World*.

From there, Jami joined a local Romance Writers of America (RWA) chapter to pen the novel. The authors in the chapter and a critique group helped Jami through the writing process. Jami knew she wasn't strong with grammar. The drive to tell a story that would bring people joy, like Susan Elizabeth Phillips had delivered, pushed Jami to fight through the process. She shared about a time her paper was red with correction marks. Jami said, "I didn't cry until I got in the car, but I cried all the way home because it was just so hard." Jami took the tears in stride. She added, "They were hard on me because they could see that I could tell a story."

It took years, but she finished the novel.

We've seen the tears. We've seen the sweat. Now we see the third piece of the idiom come to fruition—the blood. Before Jamie clocked in for work, she visited the local blood bank to sell plasma to raise money for an editor. She went as early as 4:30 a.m. because there were fewer people in line, reducing the wait time. This time I asked the big why. Why would Jami go to such an extreme?

She wrote with a purpose. "I write with the intent of making my readers' world a little bit better for a little while." She didn't want her grammar or syntax to interfere with the story. If it meant selling blood to pay for an editor, that's what she would do.

Years later, *Rock My World* would be published as *Running from a Rock Star*.

## COMPARING NOTES

How has the experience of Running from a Rock Star shaped Jami's writing process? Since then, Jami has published one novel a year. Each story goes through five rounds.

### Round One: the first draft

- Jami starts her stories with a clear beginning and end, and she has ideas for the middle.
- The raw story goes to a developmental editor.

### Round Two:

- Make edits suggested by the editor.
- Add setting and emotion.
- Self-edit to remove the cliches.
- Pull pieces to rewrite in funny or different ways.

### Round Three:

- Edit for continuity.
- Make sure the story delivers the promise.
- This process is done on a kindle where she reads and makes notes.

"I write with the intent of making my readers' world a little bit better for a little while."

**Round Four:**

- Send the book to beta readers who help her with grammar.

**Round Five:**

- Send the book to the copy/line editor.

Like all of us, Jami goes through the phases of writing. However, because she invests more time in the process, it is easy for her to fall into the mindset that the story isn't working. I asked how she knows when the story isn't working and when it's typical writer's angst.

Jami replied that at the beginning of her writing career, she shared her work with critique partners. Now a more experienced author, she draws on instinct to help her determine if her work in progress will connect with the reader. "I know I have a problem when I am writing, and I'm bored or feel like I'm rambling. I just got rid of 5,000 words or two chapters. It was like nobody was listening. Not even me. So I went back and read it and thought, 'yeah, that doesn't need to be in there.'"

Jami also shared that she'll grumble about her story, "I'll say, 'oh, this is horrible.' And my daughter will say, 'oh, you're at that point in the process.'" In other words, thinking a story is horrible is a universal reaction. Jami presses through and does her best to deliver something her readers will enjoy.

## ADVICE

Four years, several books, speaking engagements, and a podcast under her belt, Jami has accomplished yet another feat—she inspires authors. When we discussed questions she hears on the podcast, she shared that it is interesting

"Stop working on the first act of that book; like, stop editing the first act of that book because that's what a lot of us do. Get to the end. Finish the book, and then you can fix it."

# "I wanted to make people laugh and lighten their load. *I do it through writing.*"

hearing questions we've forgotten about or the answers have changed since we started writing.

I asked her to share advice she would pass along to someone trying to write their first book. Her answer, delivered in a kind, I've-been-there tone, was to get past the first act. She said, "Stop working on the first act of that book; like, stop editing the first act of that book because that's what a lot of us do. Get to the end. Finish the book, and then you can fix it." In other words, an editing loop can easily pull in the well-intentioned author. The means of extraction are simple. Move forward with the plot.

For authors later in their careers, she acknowledged that writing is still a struggle "We don't want to reach for that low hanging fruit. We're always trying to get better." To them, she said, "Don't let that cripple you." It was an aha moment where both of us stopped talking for a moment to jot a reminder.

Jami and I talked for another hour about writing, our families, and how the pandemic changed our approach to both writing and family. The conversation ended too soon, but we had to go. Our families wanted supper. Before I left my writer's desk, I wrote another Jami quote. It captures the heart of every writer and explains why she worked so hard in the beginning to share her story. "I wanted to make people laugh and lighten their load. I do it through writing." ∎

Merri Maywether

# Battling the First Draft and Winning

**D**rafting is how we get books. Books are our business. This means drafting is our business. Finishing our drafts is our top priority. No finished draft, no book. No book, no readers. The perfect first draft, that great inspired work that flows from the divine muse through us onto the page is a myth. Perfection is not our friend. Perfection is the enemy. How do we combat this enemy?

Whether we're pantsing or have made a detailed outline, we need to know where we're going. We need to know the minimum standards for what we're producing. These are the corner pieces of the puzzle that we're putting together.

- What are the minimum and maximum amount of words?
- What tropes are expected within the genre?
- What isn't tolerated in the genre?

> A first draft...is us telling ourselves the story in full for the first time.

Now, we write. Sounds simple. Yet, many of us freeze at various parts of our first draft. Some of us get obsessed with individual scenes, writing and rewriting the same few chapters. Others get distracted by the siren call of *Shiny New Thing*. Or we sit and stare at a blinking cursor because we're determined to write in linear fashion but our mind is excited about an altogether different scene. Imposter syndrome can set in, and we begin to think the story will never be good enough. For every roadblock there's a cascade of other roadblocks that we can create for ourselves to stop us finishing that first draft.

Let's discuss what a first draft is and what it isn't. A first draft is not the final product that our readers are going to get. It's us telling ourselves the story in full for the first time. Sometimes we need to tell ourselves more than what the audience will read. Or we're putting together a bare bones arc to weave other bits in later. The first draft is our foundation. Writing a first draft is a skill. Skills can be honed. We get better each time we do it because we learn what works for us.

Kevin McLaughlin's book, *You Must Write*, lays out famed writer Robert Heinlein's rules of writing. These rules date back to 1947 from a collection of essays on writing where Heinlein's article *"On the Writing of Speculative Fiction"* was first published. McLaughlin breaks each rule down into digestible chunks and discusses how each rule is relevant in the modern context.

Heinlein's rules are :

1. You must write.
2. You must finish what you start.
3. You must refrain from rewriting except to editorial order.
4. You must put it on the market.
5. You must keep it on the market until it's sold.

For the purposes of drafting, only the first three rules are relevant to us. We know we must write. Many of us have been scribbling in margins and daydreaming stories our whole lives, as writing is at the core of our beings. Focusing our writing is where we falter. Writing one story with a beginning, middle, and end can be a roller coaster of revelations and frustrations. Most of us have one story in us that we've been harboring for years trying to figure out how to tell it. Sitting down and deciding which story is ready to be told requires us to face our ego.

Writing one story with a beginning, middle, and end can be a roller coaster of revelations

McLaughlin's advice is that the tools we use, the speed we write, and even the market itself don't matter in the drafting process. We need to write. There's all kinds of organizational tools and apps to help with schedules. You can even gamify your word counts. We can use whatever tools we like to help us. If a tool doesn't work, don't use it. Tools are personal, we all have our preferences and those can change over time. Whether it's Scrivener or Google docs, at the end of the day we choose the tool that helps us get our words done.

It's shocking to think that the market doesn't matter when we write a draft. We have to remember that the first draft is not what's going to the market. The draft is us telling ourselves the story. It can be messy, grammatically and structurally. The first draft is getting it all out of our system to see what stories are there.

The speed at which we write isn't important but consistency is. Speed is another individual thing. The amount of time we carve out of our schedules for writing and how we carve that time up doesn't matter so long as we use that time to get words down. They all add up to more words and get us closer to our goal of *The End*.

Whether we're a part-time or full-time author, we decide what priority writing has in our schedule and what we can manage for regular, sustainable output. It may take some experimentation before we find a schedule that works for us. Sometimes a change is what we need in order to push through to the end.

Accountability is important in finishing a draft. Some of us need help to stay accountable. There are many techniques that indies can use to incentivize themselves to get drafts done. From setting up pre-orders to talking about our work on socials, getting the audience involved can help us stay motivated. It also helps to have another author to check in with, or a group of authors to share writing sprints and word count goals. They can provide support by cheering us on, or help by dragging us over the hurdle to our deadlines. Whether in-person or online, the indie writing community is a huge network of authors who like to help other authors.

We have to finish our draft no matter what it takes to get there. We are our own worst critics. We want to fix things right away—that backspace key is so easy to hit. Heinlein's third rule tells us to resist the urge to edit while drafting. Getting stuck in an endless editorial loop can mean we don't finish our draft. One could even argue that constant editing is the opposite of drafting. Drafting means once through to the end and then the next draft you go through it all again. In nitpicking about the small stuff, we

> **Resist the urge to edit while drafting.**

can miss the gold that is there in the draft.

Since this rule is so difficult, many writers choose to divide their drafts in chunks. They'll finish a whole chapter or a few chapters and then go back and make sure it all fits together. That means the draft of that section is done, and the author can move forward with the next batch.

After all is said and done, rules are made to be broken. Trust yourself. Trust your story. Use the vast indie network to find the people and the tools that work for you. Your drafting style is uniquely yours and what matters is that you show up for yourself and move forward with your writing journey. Finish the draft. Because only by finishing it can you publish it.

Sìne Màiri MacDougall

# Tackling the First Draft One Day at a Time

You have committed to writing a book, worked out the characters, what's going to happen to them. The world is verdant and fleshed out in your head and you're ready to write.

But fifty thousand words feels like too much. You have a fulltime job, kids to feed and nurture so they don't go feral, hobbies, friends, and that elusive unicorn called sleep.

How can anyone expect you to fit two to three thousand clean words into an already packed schedule?

The good news is that you don't have to. Writing is self-paced and best done as a part of a well-rounded life, not the center that everything else fits around. The most effective way to do this?

A daily writing habit.

> Writing is self-paced and best done as a part of a well-rounded life

## WHAT A DAILY WRITING HABIT IS NOT (NECESSARILY...)

The first exposure most people have to writing every day is National Novel Writing Month. Thousands start every November with a daily 1667 word goal so they can win the ultimate prize—completing a 50,000 word novel. And as the month progresses, the writing groups fill with stories of waking up before everyone else, trying to get words in when no one respects your time, not being able to get the right word for the sentence.

Mark Hood found himself in this situation while competing in 2019:

> "[...]November 2019 just did not go well. I missed a day or two for various reasons, and then lethargy took over. I felt that since I'd missed a day, I had to catch up. So now instead of an already challenging 1,667 words to write in a day I was faced with 3,333. Numerical symmetry aside, that's a hell of a lot of work to do."

And even though Mark stopped NaNo-WriMo 20,000 good and clean words in, the experience left him with a desire to continue writing everyday. That came by way of a challenge with one requirement—write 200 words a day.

That's less than a page in most word processing programs. Most people can complete that in 15-20 minutes. A gamification writing site like 4theWords suggests you aim for 30-45 minutes a day.

Two hundred words every day may feel like a pittance when you hear of people writing a thousand words an hour. But it's important to keep in mind that those 200 words a day will produce 73,000 words over 365 days, easily a novel and a short story that can be used as a lead magnet. Your effort and your words will add up.

Do you have more things planned for your year? Perhaps writing and saving novels for a rapid release or writing several short stories for anthologies? Doubling the goal to 400 still allows you to achieve a lot. You'd be amazed. (See chart next page.)

All of these goals are achievable and even allow for missed or low days.

But what if you've got your story finished and there's nothing on the immediate horizon?

Jess Mountifield, author of the Dragon of Shadow and Air trilogy, developed a fix that helped her write over 500 words a day for over three years. On the days that she doesn't have anything to write or she cannot muster up the energy, she writes diary style.

# OH, WHAT A DAILY WRITING HABIT CAN DO!

| Daily Goal | Monthly total (30 days) | In a month, you've written: | Yearly total (365 Days) | In a year, you've written: |
|---|---|---|---|---|
| 200 | 6,000 | Short Story OR 3 standard chapters | 73,000 | 1 - 60K novel, AND 1 - novella |
| 444* | 13,320 | 2 - 6500 word anthology shorts OR over 4 standard chapters | 162,060 | 2 - 60K novels and some short stories OR 1 - epic fantasy |
| 500 | 15,000 | 2 - 7500 words anthology shorts OR 5 standard chapters | 182,500 | 3 - 60K novels OR 2 - 90K novels OR 1 - epic fantasy OR You wrote the entire short story anthology yourself. (24 - 7500 word shorts) |
| 1,000 | 30,000 | A short novel | 365,000 | 6 - 60K novels OR 4 - 90K novels OR 1 - epic fantasy with an appendix |

* Daily Goal in 4thewords.com

Writing daily is not about how many words you can write, it's about developing a disciplined and consistent habit.

"Allowing myself to write diary style snippets kept me coming back each day even when life was hard," she states in a post on Facebook.

"These days were usually when I was stuck on plot, exhausted from the tiny humans, or in between books. Sometimes I did these to get into writing and then still wrote a decent amount afterwards."

"The first year," Mountfield continues, "I wrote 60k+ of diary style entries. The second year 10k roughly. The third year, I think I've maybe done it a handful of times."

Depending on your schedule, a fixed word count may not be the way to go. But you may have a certain period of time, such as your children's nap time, a lunch break, or your commute (if you're the driver, check out our article on dictation).

Snatching moments of time is a low pressure way to pull the story from your head to the page. And they're also linked to something that happens most days, making it easier to make it a habit.

Another benefit to using a timed session instead of a word count is the internal editor tends to quiet down when faced with a ticking clock. Try it yourself: set a timer for five minutes or go against Vi the Sprint Creature in 4thewords.com, then write the next section of your story. You'll be surprised how many words come out of you when you have to keep typing for five minutes in order to win.

> "Allowing myself to write diary style snippets kept me coming back each day even when life was hard,"

Month  Year

**Mar**

| F | S | S | | M | T | W | T | F | S | S |
|---|---|---|---|---|---|---|---|---|---|---|
| 5 | 6 | 7 | | 1 | 2 | 3 | 4 | 5 | 6 | 7 |
| 12 | 13 | 14 | | 8 | 9 | 10 | 11 | 12 | 13 | 14 |
| 19 | 20 | 21 | | 15 | 16 | 17 | 18 | 19 | 20 | 21 |
| 26 | 27 | 28 | | 22 | 23 | 24 | 25 | 26 | 27 | 28 |
| | | | | 29 | 30 | 31 | | | | |

**Jun**

| F | S | S | | M | T | W | T | F | S | S |
|---|---|---|---|---|---|---|---|---|---|---|
| | 1 | 2 | | | 1 | 2 | 3 | 4 | 5 | 6 |
| 7 | 8 | 9 | | 7 | 8 | 9 | 10 | 11 | 12 | 13 |
| 14 | 15 | 16 | | 14 | 15 | 16 | 17 | 18 | 19 | 20 |
| 21 | 22 | 23 | | 21 | 22 | 23 | 24 | 25 | 26 | 27 |
| 28 | 29 | 30 | | 28 | 29 | 30 | | | | |

**Sep**

| F | S | S | | M | T | W | T | F | S | S |
|---|---|---|---|---|---|---|---|---|---|---|
| | | 1 | | | | 1 | 2 | 3 | 4 | 5 |
| 6 | 7 | 8 | | 6 | 7 | 8 | 9 | 10 | 11 | 12 |
| 13 | 14 | 15 | | 13 | 14 | 15 | 16 | 17 | 18 | 19 |
| 20 | 21 | 22 | | 20 | 21 | 22 | 23 | 24 | 25 | 26 |
| 27 | 28 | 29 | | 27 | 28 | 29 | 30 | | | |

**Dec**

| F | S | S | | M | T | W | T | F | S | S |
|---|---|---|---|---|---|---|---|---|---|---|
| 5 | 6 | 7 | | | | 1 | 2 | 3 | 4 | 5 |
| 12 | 13 | 14 | | 6 | 7 | 8 | 9 | 10 | 11 | 12 |
| 19 | 20 | 21 | | 13 | 14 | 15 | 16 | 17 | 18 | 19 |
| 26 | 27 | 28 | | 20 | 21 | 22 | 23 | 24 | 25 | 26 |
| | | | | 27 | 28 | 29 | 30 | 31 | | |

...ars                                    Inbox

## WHAT A DAILY WRITING HABIT IS - CONSISTENCY.

Writing daily is not about how many words you can write, it's about developing a disciplined and consistent habit.

The goal of this habit is not to rack up high numbers. The aim is to write a little bit until you finish your chapter, then the next, until you have a complete novel. Starting out, a full novel can seem like a daunting task, but with a daily writing habit, it doesn't have to be. Finish your rough draft one day at a time, and watch how your word count grows. ■

Chrishaun Keller-Hanna

# Dictating Your Way to a First Draft

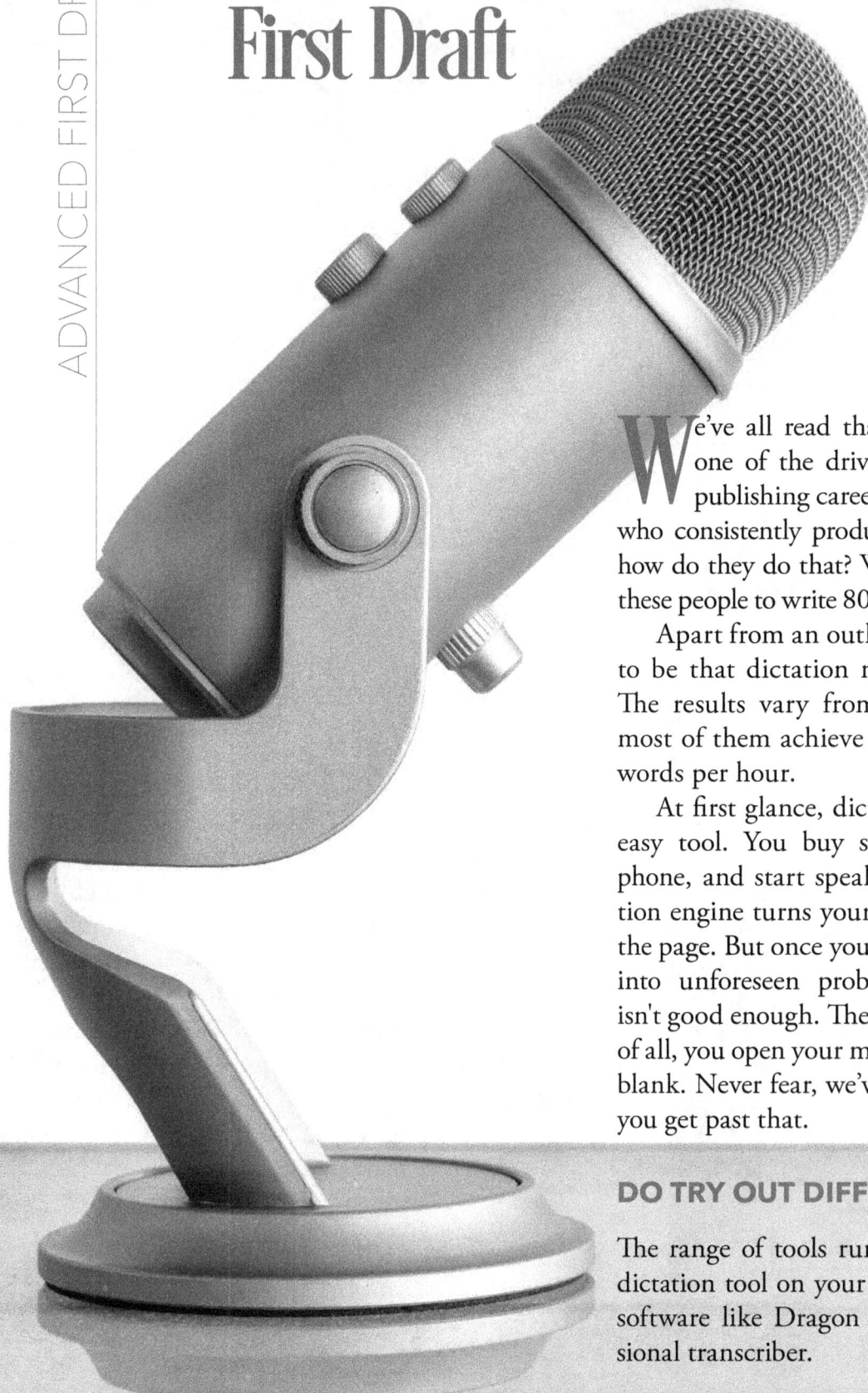

We've all read that publishing fast can be one of the drivers for a successful indie publishing career. In fact, there are writers who consistently produce a book a month. But how do they do that? What single factor enables these people to write 80,000 words in four weeks?

Apart from an outline, the consensus seems to be that dictation makes all the difference. The results vary from author to author, but most of them achieve between 3,000 to 5,000 words per hour.

At first glance, dictation seems to be a very easy tool. You buy some software, a microphone, and start speaking while the transcription engine turns your words into sentences on the page. But once you get started, you may run into unforeseen problems. Your microphone isn't good enough. The software lags. And worst of all, you open your mouth and your mind goes blank. Never fear, we've got some tricks to help you get past that.

## DO TRY OUT DIFFERENT METHODS

The range of tools runs from using an inbuilt dictation tool on your PC or Mac to dedicated software like Dragon or even hiring a professional transcriber.

> **You might be shocked as to how different speaking your prose feels compared to typing it.**

There are several free options you can use to evaluate if dictation might be for you. For example, Google Docs Voice Typing via Chrome allows you to speak directly into your document. Windows 10 has a speech recognition feature included on your PC. Apple offers the same with Apple Dictation. The accuracy of the free dictation engines are improving all the time, but predictably, a paid application will produce better results.

The most often used software, Dragon Professional Individual 15, can be expensive, but there are deals throughout the year that make the cost more palatable. It even allows you

to dictate into your phone or a dictaphone while you're away from your desk. Once you return home, the software will transcribe directly into your document. It feels like magic, watching words appear on your screen.

There are some free mobile phone apps worth mentioning. Google's Gboard app works with both Android and iOS and is very fast, albeit not that accurate. The Otter app offers 600 free minutes per month. You can send a link of your recording to collaborators and export both text and audio.

The last and most expensive option in the long run is a human transcriber. Rates range from

$0.90 to $1.25 and more per minute. At a dictation rate of 3,000 words per hour, this would cost you $1,080 to $1,500 for a 60,000 word novel.

Each option has its pros and cons, and you won't know what you like until you try it. Once you decide to go ahead, you might be shocked as to how different speaking your prose feels compared to typing it.

## DON'T WORRY ABOUT HOW DIFFERENT IT FEELS

Maybe it's a cliche to tell you that it's all in your head, but that doesn't make it any less true. When writers moved from handheld pens to typewriters, the process felt just as uncomfortable and awkward. It's literally a matter of practice.

The biggest obstacle for anybody trying dictation is that it's so much faster than typing. Your brain needs to be trained to structure your thoughts a bit differently.

Therefore, DON'T freak out if your dictation doesn't flow as it would if you were typing by hand. That's perfectly normal and improves with practice.

DO learn a few commands, such as "period," "comma," or "new line." Within a few minutes, you will be so used to them, you won't need to pause to insert punctuation.

DON'T speak your quotation marks, though. That will slow down your dialogue, and it stops it from flowing naturally.

Pro Tip: Don't bother teaching your software unusual names. Replace your fantasy character's name with John and do a search-replace throughout the finished document.

## DON'T GET HUNG UP ON DETAILS

Another key obstacle for many people is that they're away from their desk and their research. They can't check timelines, or details of settings, or what the eye color of the character is. This shouldn't stop you.

DO tag your text by using spoken placeholders, like "insert eye color here." The same method works extremely well when you get stuck on any other detail. The key advantage of dictation is to get your first draft down as quickly as possible.

DON'T hesitate to say, "insert fight scene here," or "describe inner city bustle here." Details can be filled in later.

## DO BE CREATIVE WHEN YOU'RE STUCK

Every dictating writer is familiar with getting stuck in mid-flow. Your brain gets confused, and no words emerge from your mouth that make any sense. This is common and easily solved.

DO dare to improvise. Imagine you're telling the story to a friend. Act out your character's voice. Babble about something completely different for a few seconds until your "speaker's block" resolves itself. All your ramblings will be cut when you return to your document.

Sometimes, however, despite your best efforts, the dictating conditions aren't ideal. Maybe you have an unusual accent.

**Dare to improvise**

## The objective is to get the story down first.

Or there's a lot of background noise, and the recording is jumbled. Unfortunately, this happens.

### BUT WHEN IT DOES, DON'T GIVE UP ON DICTATION

Even if you look at your document, and you can barely make sense of the transcription, don't despair. Listen back to your recording and correct any mistakes the software made. It is a tedious process and can take as long as speaking the text in the first place, but you can't edit a blank page. Even though the accuracy might only be 80%, you will still be editing a piece of your writing that didn't exist before you spoke it.

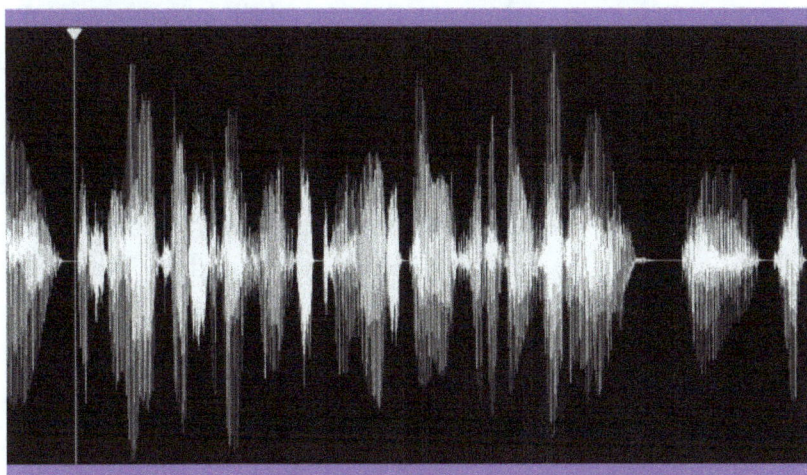

## THE MINDSET OF DICTATION

A fabulous book that deals with exactly this topic is *Foolproof Dictation* by Christoper Downing. He was kind enough to contribute some of his insights to this article.

DON'T expect your sentences to come out fully formed.

DO have some kind of outline. Even if you're more comfortable writing into the void, for dictation you need at least a few bullet points to guide you along the scene.

DON'T expect to have a clean first draft when you're dictating. Chris calls it the "sloppy first draft." If you get stuck, summarize. Don't be afraid to tell instead of show. The objective is to get the story down first. "Showing" can be added in the edits.

Chris suggests to start with small, incremental periods of dictation. Try two or five minutes. The key skill to learn is consistency. Work your way up. Once you're used to showing up daily, you can expand the amount of time you spend dictating.

He uses a great exercise with his coaching clients. They are encouraged to keep a narrative journal which they add to daily. Chris emphasizes the importance of it being a non-pressure activity. Nobody but you will hear your ramblings.

Use the journal to explore different narrative avenues. Maybe speak a scene using only dialogue. Create different plotlines. This is not supposed to be your work in progress, but a daily exercise to make your brain feel comfortable with dictation.

With this kind of practice, you will be amazed at how much more comfortable you'll get with speaking your first draft. Writing first drafts can feel daunting and take longer than you thought. Dictation may be just the tool to get you to The End. Plus, as an added benefit, you'll spend some time away from your desk. What's not to like? Give it a try! ▪

Marion Hermannsen

# TACKLING A FIRST DRAFT CAN BE A DAUNTING EXPERIENCE. WE ASKED THE INDIE AUTHOR COMMUNITY FOR THE BEST TIPS ON WRITING AND/OR FINISHING A FIRST DRAFT.

Find those around you who will encourage you, always. Once you've got your crew, you can get through anything.

I AM a writer, publisher, consultant, and audio proofer of sci-fi, military sci-fi, and gamelit stories

**Dawn Chapman**
https://dawnchapmanauthor.com/ .

Just write. Sit. And. Write. Make the words come out, even when you don't want to. Having the discipline to get the first draft done is what separates a hobbyist from a professional. It's a lot easier to edit a page of writing than a blank one.

I AM from the wild and windswept moors of Yorkshire, England. I write epic fantasy as Meg Cowley and British crime thrillers as Meg Jolly.

**Meg Jolly**
www.megcowley.com
www.megjolly.com

For me, knowing my ending. It gives you a goal to shoot towards and an ending to resolve itself, so that even when you're in the middle and slogging, you can tell that you're making progress.

I AM a LitRPG & xianxia author who delves in short stories and novels in fantastic worlds, often influenced by my love of martial arts and history. I am the author of the bestselling series the System Apocalypse, A Thousand Li and other great scifi and fantasy series.

**Tao Wong**
https://mylifemytao.com

Find someone who will always be your #1 fan on the roughest days, and write for them.

I AM a trauma survivor who writes stories to help people like me heal.

**Sheryl Recinos**
https://sherylrecinosmd.com

A preorder. Nothing else seems to work. I have no problem breaking promises to myself or others (as there are no real life consequences), but for some reason, preorders do it for me. The nagging emails. The public shaming to my readers. Shiver…

I AM a paranormal romance writer who hates to make her heroine choose. I will always deliver a happy ending, even though I put my characters through hell to get there.

**Ella J. Smyth**
https://ellajsmyth.com

*The Writing On The Wall:*

# Getting to know Scrivener

**Think of housing your project in a digital three-ring binder and you've got a good idea of how the Binder works.**

When writing your novel, you want a program that can contain all the amazing ideas that are swirling around in your brain in one place. Literature & Latte's Scrivener is designed to do just that. More than just a word processor, it provides a place to plot your novel, write it, hold all your research, and get it ready for publication. It's a powerhouse of a program, but despite its many features new users don't need to be overwhelmed. The basic functions are easy to grasp, allowing you to start writing without worrying about some of the more advanced features.

## OVERVIEW

The main view of Scrivener is divided into three sections, the Binder, the Document, and the Inspector. Think of housing your project in a digital three-ring binder and you've got a good idea of how the **Binder** works. You can divide your project into chapters and parts, each containing as many scenes as required. The Binder also houses templates for characters and settings, research folders, front matter, and notes. This allows you to keep all of the information related to your project in one place. There is also a Trash folder, so if you decide to delete a chapter or scene, it doesn't vanish immediately.

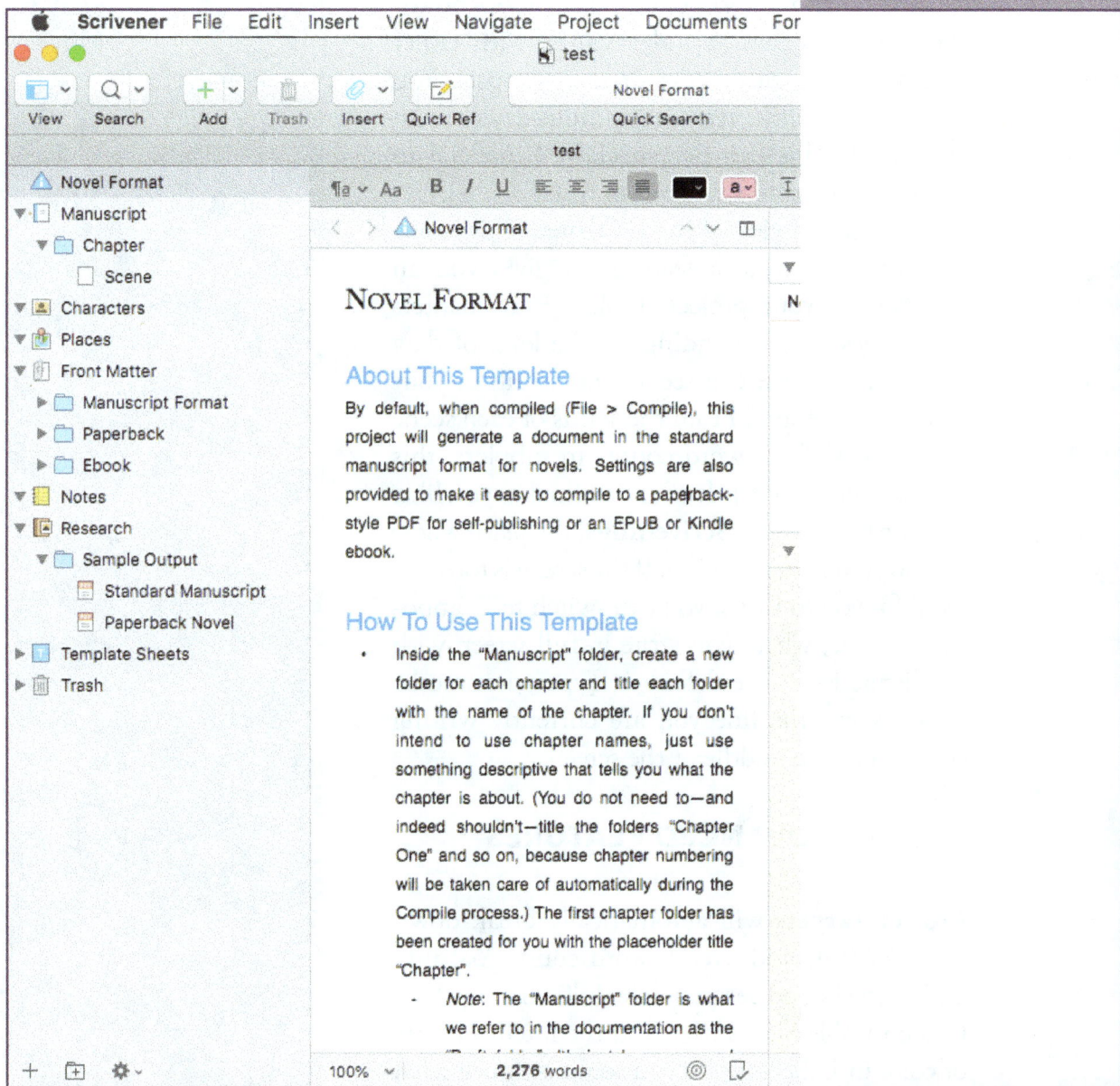

On the right hand side of the screen is the **Inspector**. The Inspector panel provides space for comments, bookmarks, story goals, or notes. You can add keywords, custom metadata, and labels. It also allows you to assign each scene a status so you know if it's been written, edited, or still to do.

The middle portion of the screen, the **Document**, has three separate views: Scrivenings, Outliner, and Corkboard. The **Corkboard** shows your scenes as index cards, with either a preview of written text or the synopsis. You can easily shuffle the cards around as much as needed. This can be especially beneficial to those who tend to write out of order.

The second view is the **Outliner**. This is one of Scrivener's greatest features. It gives you an overview of your project, broken into chapters and scenes. But depending on the level of data you've added, you can see all the details of your project in one spot. From the status of each scene to the POV, from word counts to subplots, this view can be as in depth or as minimal as you like.

The final view is **Scrivenings**, the place where you do your actual writing. If the screen is too cluttered for you to focus, you can switch to Composition mode, where you write in full screen with no distractions. The default is Typewriter mode, which keeps the line you are currently writing centered in the middle of the screen.

## ADVANCED FEATURES

**Project Targets** will automatically break down your deadline and overall word count goal into daily targets and let you schedule writing days. Customizable Status tags, and the intelligent use of color in Label tags let you see at a glance what needs to be drafted, edited, or sent to a critique partner. The history function shows you how many words you've written each day and month.

You can save story structures as **templates,** or import ones that others have created e.g. Save the Cat, or the W-plot. Templates can also be used for marketing checklists, release plans, and favorite story-structuring tools.

In theory, Scrivener can **integrate** with Grammarly or ProWritingAid to check spelling and grammar as you write. However, some authors have reported that ProWritingAid caused issues with their document, so if this is a critical feature for you, test how robust these integrations are for you and your usage during the trial period. If you use Plottr (featured in last month's Technology article), it can output directly to Scrivener, so your plot points are lined up ready to start writing. Scapple, also by Literature & Latte, allows you to drag and drop your mindmaps directly into Scrivener.

Scrivener has a few advanced functions for revising your book as well. The first is the **Snapshot** feature, which allows you to take a "snapshot" of your document now, and later compare any changes you may have made. **Segmentation** allows you to slice and label snippets of text, and reorder the labelled snippets, scenes, and chapters using the Binder, Corkboard, or Outliner.

**Project Targets will automatically break down your deadline and overall word count goal into daily targets and let you schedule writing days.**

**PRO-TIP**

Scrivener on the Mac will NOT create a print quality pdf that you need to create a paperback/hardcover with IngramSpark. This has to do with pdf formats and the Mac operating system. LibreOffice will create one from the docx Scrivener compiles.

## CREATING YOUR OUTPUT FILE

**Compile** lets you create a long list of file types including word processor (rtf, docx, doc, odt for Open Office), ebook (epub2, epub3, mobi with KindleGen which has been phased out), and pdf formats.

Pro-tip: Scrivener on the Mac will NOT create a print quality pdf that you need to create a paperback/hardcover with IngramSpark. This has to do with pdf formats and the Mac operating system. LibreOffice will create one from the docx Scrivener compiles.

Gwen Hernandez, author of *Scrivener For Dummies*, says, "The new version of Compile is both a reason that people get a little freaked out, but it also—once you understand how it works—is way more flexible and it has better capabilities." The new Section Types and Section Layouts let you define the formatting and content separately. This means the Compile function is still complex, but the set-up is customizable and reusable.

Print
PDF

Rich Text (.rtf)
Rich Text with Attachments (.rtfd)
Microsoft Word (.docx)
Microsoft Word 97-2004 (.doc)
OpenOffice (.odt)

✓ Plain Text (.txt)
Web Page (.html)

Final Draft (.fdx)
Fountain Screenplay (.fountain)

ePub 3 Ebook (.epub)
ePub 2 Ebook (.epub)
Kindle KF8/Mobi Ebook (.mobi)
Kindle Mobi Ebook (.mobi)

MultiMarkdown
MultiMarkdown → LaTeX (.tex)
MultiMarkdown → OpenOffice (.odt)
MultiMarkdown → Web Page (.html)
MultiMarkdown → Flat XML (.fodt)

## VERSION 3

Scrivener3 was recently released for the Windows operating system. The newest Windows version has finally caught up to the Mac version released three years ago.

The new release supports 64 bit processing, making the program faster and more stable. System requirements can be found on Literature & Latte's website.

Version 3 has more editing bells & whistles including:

- **Linguistic Focus** - highlights dialogue or adverbs, so you can check your style.
- **Threaded notecards** - group scenes together.

The "thread" is based on the Label and only one Label is allowed per scene or chunk of text. That means you can't use the threads to show the connections between story threads. The feature does work for keeping track of point-of-view characters, but so do the color-coded Labels in the Binder.

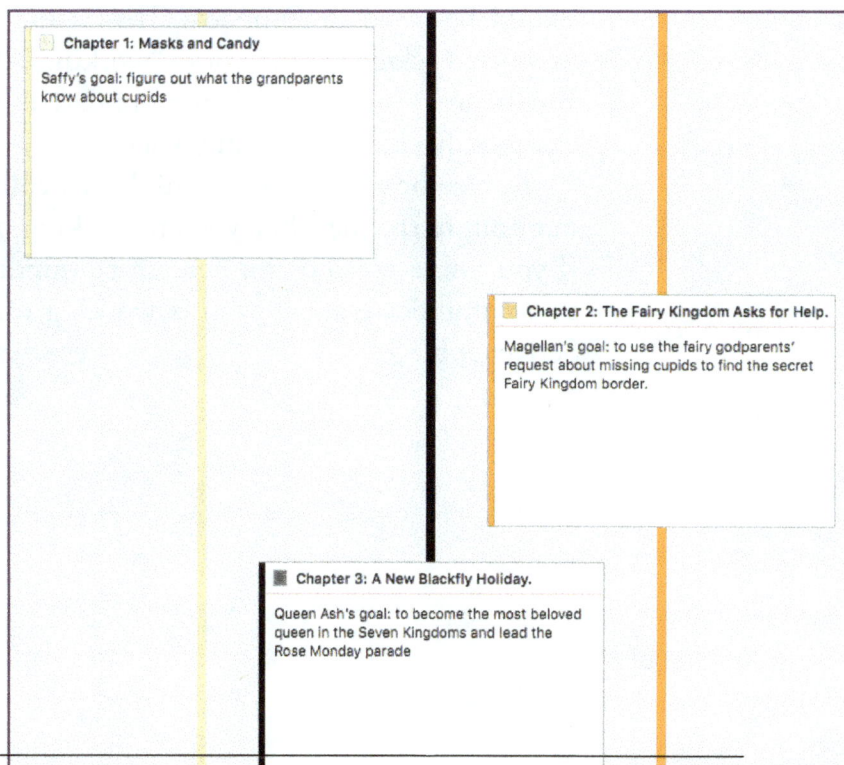

Chapter 1: Masks and Candy

Saffy's goal: figure out what the grandparents know about cupids

Chapter 2: The Fairy Kingdom Asks for Help.

Magellan's goal: to use the fairy godparents' request about missing cupids to find the secret Fairy Kingdom border.

Chapter 3: A New Blackfly Holiday.

Queen Ash's goal: to become the most beloved queen in the Seven Kingdoms and lead the Rose Monday parade

## PRICING

Scrivener is a one-time purchase, currently priced at $49 USD. The Scrivener license covers all devices in your household on the same platform. If you have both Mac and Windows, you will need a separate license for each (available as a discounted bundle). There is also a generous 30-day free trial period, which lets you see if Scrivener is for you. This isn't just 30 calendar days from when you start your trial period—Scrivener only counts the days you use the software, supporting your schedule.

Pro-tip for switching devices. "Close the project on your laptop and let it finish updating. Make sure you have an internet connection. Once the update is complete, you can open the file on another device. The "working copy" should be saved in Dropbox. This is the only supported cloud service for "working" files, which are constantly being updated with changes. Backups can go anywhere.

Remember, Scrivener doesn't lock a collaborator out of the file while you are working on it. If you give a collaborator access, it's important to communicate about who is working on the Scrivener file."

## SUMMARY

Scrivener's strongest feature is its customization. From changing your general text options as you write, to metadata, labels, and view, to compiling output options, you can make it work for you. There are a lot of resources to help you get started; from video tutorials and the user forums on Literature and Latte's website, to free courses from Gwen Hernandez for both Windows and Mac users. If Scrivener matches your drafting or editing style, its powerful "heavy drafting" tools can be valuable on their own. If you want to use Compile to format ebooks and print books as well, it's definitely worth exploring. ■

Laurel Decher

## PRO-TIP

When switching devices: Close the project on your laptop and let it finish updating. Make sure you have an internet connection. Once the update is complete, you can open the file on another device. The "working copy" should be saved in Dropbox. This is the only supported cloud service for "working" files, which are constantly being updated with changes. Backups can go anywhere.

Remember, Scrivener doesn't lock a collaborator out of the file while you are working on it. If you give a collaborator access, it's important to communicate about who is working on the Scrivener file.

—Gwen Hernandez, author of *Scrivener For Dummies*

# Tech Tools

Courtesy of IndieAuthorTools.com
Got a tool you love and want to share with us?
Submit a tool at IndieAuthorTools.com

| | | |
|---|---|---|
| **ScribeCount** *Numbers From Your Words* | **SCRIBE COUNT** | All the data you need to keep track of, in one central location. This author services company provides sales reporting, ad tracking, social media management, marketing and analytics tools, and news aggregation, all in one real-time easy to read platform.<br><br>indieauthortools.com/scribecount-2 |
| **4THEWORDS** | **4 THE WORDS** | Meeting word count goals can be daunting. 4 The Words is an adventure game that helps you accomplish your goals without even realizing it. This online writing game was designed to push your daily word count and to help you maintain a consistent writing habit.<br><br>indieauthortools.com/4thewords |
| | **PAYMO** | The swiss army knife of project management. And yet - it's a little bit more. Use it for project management, time tracking, pomodoro timing, and make use of the handy financial integrations.<br><br>indieauthortools.com/paymo |
| | **REV VOICE RECORDER** | Be ready when inspiration strikes. The Rev Voice Recorder is an app for your phone that pairs convenient voice recording with simple transcription services. It provides superior sound quality, user-friendly functionality, and quick transcription services all at your fingertips.<br><br>indieauthortools.com/rev-voice-recorder |
| **Audiate®** | **AUDIATE** | You can't hit backspace on spoken words… or can you? Audiate makes editing recorded audio as simple as editing typed or written documents. Become your own audio engineer and edit your audio by editing the text transcriptions generated from your dictations.<br><br>indieauthortools.com/audiate |

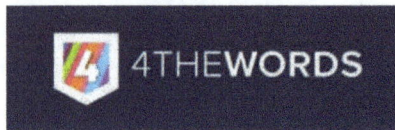

# AUTHOR LOGOS:
## MAKING YOUR MARK

A logo is an asset that every author should consider having in their marketing repertoire. Your logo will be one of the key indicators of your brand. It will be one of the first things readers see when visiting your website or your social media profiles. When deciding on your logo, ask yourself whether it will help your brand achieve its purpose. For an author, that purpose is usually to sell more books to the right readers.

Whether you make your own logo or work with a designer to create one for you, there are a number of things you should consider, such as branding, genre (including use of fonts), taglines, how to work with a designer, and a few legal questions.

### BRANDING

One of the first things to consider when designing a logo is that it should be "on brand." Think about your author brand and its purpose. What do you want to achieve with your brand? Who do you want to be in readers' eyes? How do you want them to remember you? What are you known for, as an author? Do you always write a certain type of character? Do you tend to use a certain setting? Maybe you're drawn to a certain trope? These are important questions to consider even before you sit down to create your logo or hire a designer.

> Who do you want to be in readers' eyes?

Once you've answered these questions, consider creating a brand board. A brand board is a short cheat sheet containing the visual elements of your brand: fonts, patterns, colors. Using these elements on your website and your social media will help create a cohesive, unified look across all of your platforms. Why would you want a unified look? When you enter a store or a restaurant (such as Zara or McDonald's) anywhere in the world, the interior is instantly recognizable. You want to stir that same feeling of familiarity and comfort within readers. You want them to immediately know that they're visiting one of your pages.

Building a brand board can be daunting. If you're having trouble, ask yourself whether there is a color that you would like your author brand to be associated with. (Remember that different colors convey different emotions.) That color is a good starting point to help build your brand board. A good designer can also create a brand board for you, either before they work on your logo, simultaneously, or even afterward. This is known as a "brand package" or "brand design."

## GENRE

The same principles of genre apply to logos as they do to covers. Romance authors may wish to use cursive fonts with red or pink detailing. Sci-fi authors may wish to use sans serif fonts and clean lines. Fantasy authors, on the other hand, could use bold, serif fonts with a medieval feel and fantastical elements (such as dragons or swords). Look at your bestselling book covers. What is it about them that makes them striking? Are there any elements you could adapt and incorporate into your logo?

## TAGLINES

It may be a good idea to include a short tagline in your logo. A simple descriptive term such as "romance author" would do. Or, you could get creative and think of something that will convey to readers exactly the kind of stories you write. For example: "Fairy tales with a twist" or "Small town love stories with cowboys, ranches, and happily-ever-afters."

## WORKING WITH A DESIGNER

Hiring a designer is a great way to quickly get a high-quality logo that will convey genre and the purpose of your author brand. Designers may often help you when you're stuck for ideas. There are, however, certain things you should think about before hiring a designer.

For instance, should you give a designer full creative freedom for your project, or should you give them a detailed checklist of requirements?

The answers depend on a number of things.

Designers are creatives, and creatives often enjoy interpreting briefs on their own and showing their creative flare. The risk with this is that they may miss the mark and not cater to your needs, especially if the designer hasn't worked with authors before.

However, there are designers who prefer to get an in-depth brief with specific details and examples (fonts, stock images). These designers prefer for their clients to state exactly what they want. This may also be appropriate in instances where you feel that the designer's skills are solid, but they might not have worked with authors or your genre before. If you know exactly what

**ROBYN'S BOARD**

*your* **BRAND COLORS**

565E5A  DFC2D1  ACA4B6  B8B4B9  2D2D4D

*alternate* **LOGOS & WATERMARK**

*inspiration* **& STYLE**

*brand* **FONTS**

*Boulders Beach Script*

**BOULDERS BEACH SERIF**

*brand* **PATTERNS**

you want and you won't be happy with anything other than what's in your head, giving a designer a detailed briefing and checklist may be the way to go. Remember though, that if you go with this option, you're not giving your designer the chance to be creative.

That said, if you have a vague idea of what you want, the middle ground may be the most viable option for you. Create a checklist of elements you want your logo to contain, but don't show it to your designer just yet. Tell them what you want, but allow them to be creative first—they may surprise you and present you with something you didn't know you wanted.

## A NOTE ON THE LEGAL SIDE

Not all stock sites allow for stock images to be registered as trademarks. (A trademark grants the owner a right for that mark to be used in commerce. It's a right for that mark to be used commercially on goods or within services.) It's best to read the terms and conditions in detail before using stock images in a logo that you intend to register. What's even better in this situation? Hiring a designer who will draw/illustrate

Ella J. Smyth

*your* **BRAND COLORS**

035477  9C569D  171B28  E2AFBE  6295B2

*alternate* **LOGOS & WATERMARK**

Ella J. Smyth
UNAPOLOGETIC ROMANCES

*inspiration* **& STYLE**

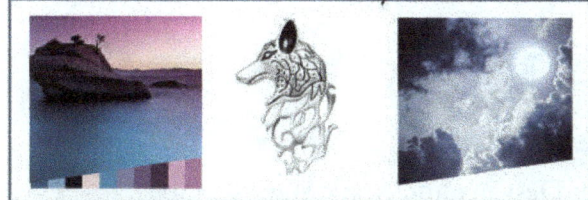

*brand* **FONTS**

CINZEL | Candara

*brand* **PATTERNS**

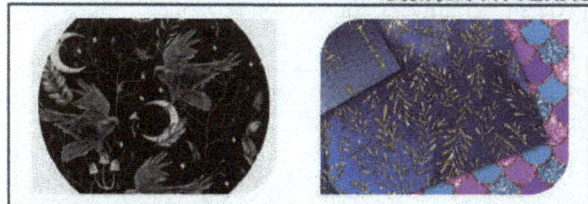

Bonus content: Get your own brand board template on the website here: https://writelink.to/ynxcl4

your logo for you from scratch. But be sure to let your designer know that you intend to register the logo as a trademark and that you intended to use it for commercial purposes. This may require special permission from the designer. When in doubt, speak to your designer.

What about font licensing? If you're creating your own logo, make sure that you buy a font license that covers commercial use. When working with a designer, it won't hurt to double check with your designer that they are indeed using fonts with commercial use licenses. Take a look on creativemarket.com or myfonts.com for inspiration and to find that perfect font!

## CONCLUSION

There are many elements to consider when it comes to designing an eye-catching author logo that will sell your books to the right readers. Does it convey genre? Have you used genre-appropriate fonts and elements? Will readers get a feel for your stories by looking at your logo? Does it fit your brand? Once you've considered all the elements in this article, go forth and create that perfect author logo! ■

Kasia Lasinska

# Podcasts We Love

## THE REBEL AUTHOR PODCAST

Hosted by Sacha Black

A motivational show for all the creatives out there with an inner rebel. Listen for interviews, industry news, tips, tricks and tools to help you take your creative business to the next level.

https://writelink.to/x84wuh

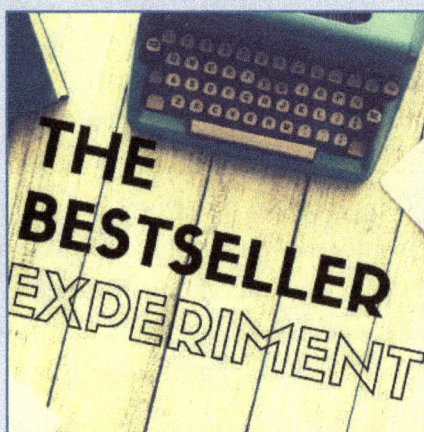

## THE BESTSELLER EXPERIMENT

Hosted by Mark Desvaux and Mark Stay

Join the two Marks in their weekly podcast as they talk with leading lights from the publishing industry, million-selling, chart-topping authors who collectively have sold over half a billion books!

https://writelink.to/8dtqeh

## THE CREATIVE SHIFT

Hosted by Dan Blank

Interviews with writers and artists who have doubled-down on their creative vision. The focus is on deeper questions such as how we make decisions, deal with anxiety, the habits and routines that matter, and the reality of what it looks like to be a full-time creative professional.

https://writelink.to/oy0qdz

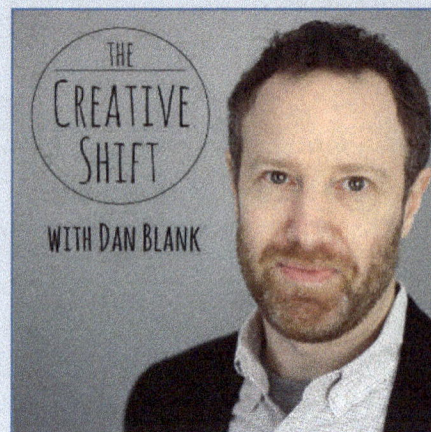

# Devil in the Details:

## KILL OR CURE?

**A**lfred Hitchcock famously said, "I think everyone enjoys a nice murder, provided he is not the victim." In reality, there is no such thing as a nice murder or a perfect murder but, in writing, there can be the "right" murder. The death that best suits the victim's or killer's character, situation, motives, and place in time.

The method of death should always be an important consideration and the answers to the following questions will help you satisfy the reader's curiosity.

- Is it viewed as a mercy killing?
- Does the killer want to exact revenge?
- Is it a murder of convenience?
- Will it be a messy, violent crime of passion or a cold, calculated remote affair?
- What resources does the killer have available?
- Do they need special access or a certain skill or knowledge?

These questions become even more pertinent when choosing death by poison.

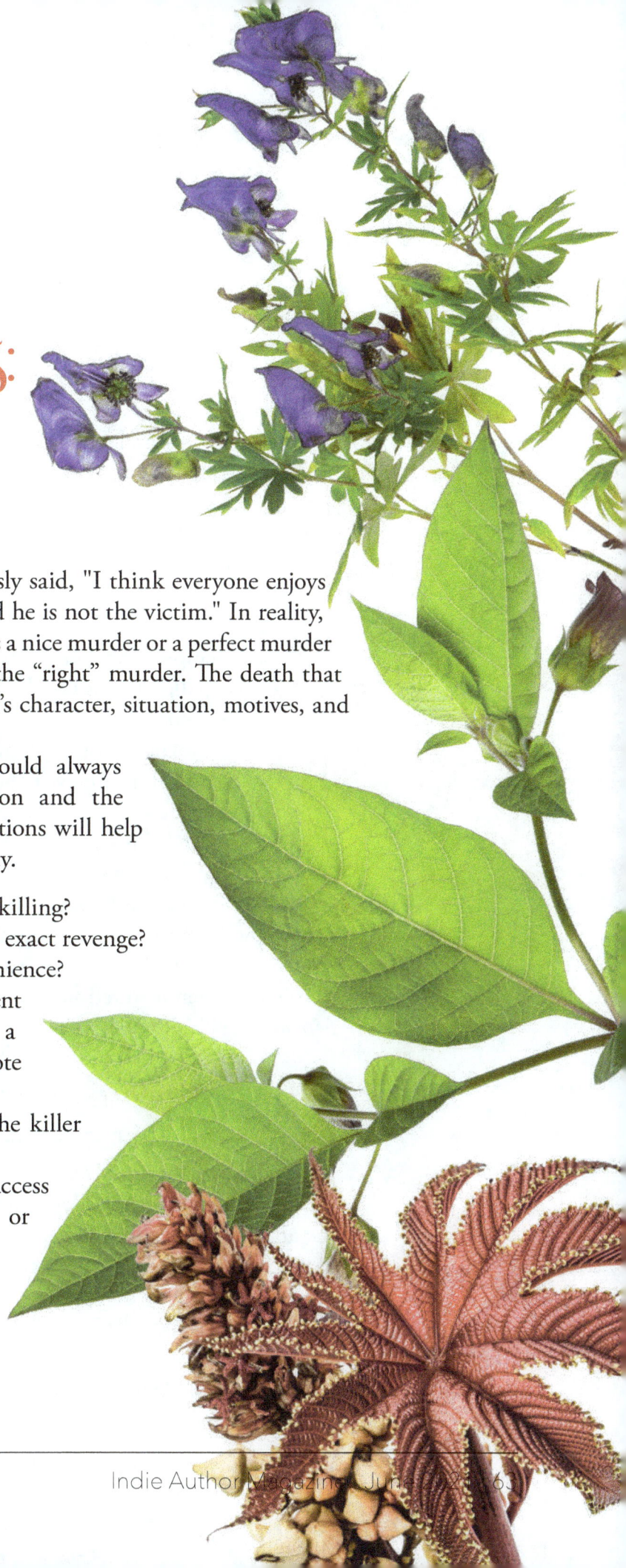

## DETAILS GONE WRONG

The wicked wonders of the natural world offer a veritable cornucopia of potential murder weapons for murder mystery, historical ,and fantasy stories, but it is vital to get the details right. The bottom line is research, research, research. No one is immune to being called out on their mistakes. John Boyne, author of *The Boy in the Striped Pyjamas*, admitted to falling foul of a bad Google search. In *A Traveller at the Gates of Wisdom*, he accidentally included monsters from the video game *The Legend of Zelda: Breath of the Wild*. In one now notorious paragraph, there's an attempt to poison Attila the Hun, using "Octorok eyeball," "the tail of the red lizalfos and four Hylian shrooms."

Boyne's mistake confused modern-day fantasy with historical accuracy. If he had cross-checked his source with a few credible reference books, he could have easily avoided this mistake. At the opposite end of the scale, Queen of Mystery, Agatha Christie, is often cited for her specialist insight into poisons. Christie worked as a hospital pharmacist and was an avid student her entire life, though even she was not averse to inventing toxic substances when it suited her story, for example, in *The Mirror Crack'd*.

> The wicked wonders of the natural world offer a veritable cornucopia of potential murder weapons for murder mysteries, historical and fantasy stories

## REAL LIFE INSPIRATION

Real-life crime is a useful source for ideas. Ben Hubbard's *Poison: The History of Potions, Powders and Murderous Practitioners* is a shiny illustrated collection of historical poisonings from the ancient world through to the twenty-first century (Anthrax, Polonium-210, Dioxin, etc). Or you could check out *Death in the Garden: Poisonous Plants and Their Use Throughout History* by Michael Brown, which includes color photographs, historical uses, Latin names, and common names. For useful cultivation and

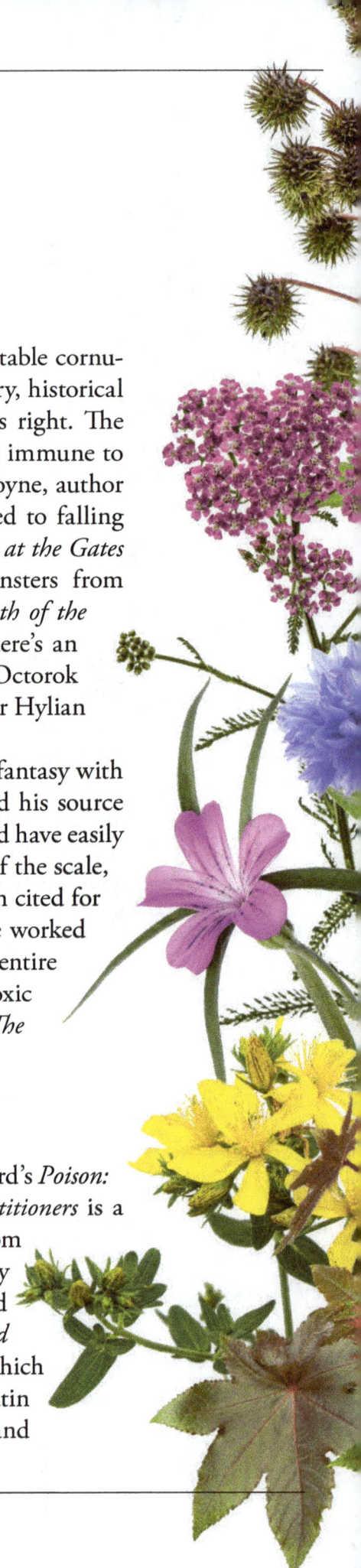

geographical details, with the feel of a Victorian sketchbook, consider Amy Stewart's *Wicked Plants: The A-Z of Plants That Maim, Intoxicate and Otherwise Offend*. Stewart's book revels in the graphic details of the unfortunate effects of these innocent-looking flora.

As Renaissance physician and toxicologist Paracelsus (1493-1541) asserted, "Poison is in everything, and no thing is without poison. The dosage makes it either a poison or a remedy." Perhaps your writing needs some magical potions rooted in folklore or ancient wisdom? The common dandelion is a remedy for warts. Wild fennel seeds can relieve indigestion, flatulence, and hiccups and, when boiled in wine, are an antidote to eating poisoned mushrooms. In the Second World War, medics on all sides used garlic as an antiseptic. Dracula wouldn't do very well in the trenches.

*Witch's Garden: Plants in Folklore, Magic and Traditional Medicine* by Sandra Lawrence is full of interesting facts about the historic use of healing herbs. For example, Britain changed its calendar from the old "Julian" style to the Gregorian version in 1752, which explains why certain traditions such as Midsummer and Christmas now seem slightly out of step with Mother Nature. This is important to know if you are relying on a plant flowering at a certain point in your historically murderous plot.

As a letter sent to Agatha Christie in 1975 illustrates, getting it right can even save lives. A South American woman wrote to her how she had recognised a wife was using thallium to poison her husband after reading *The Pale Horse*. She alerted the police and the man survived. The devil is indeed in the detail. ■

Susan Odev

> This is important to know if you are relying on a plant flowering at a certain point in your historically murderous plot.

# Urban Fantasy Tropes

**W**hat makes a book an *urban fantasy* and not merely *contemporary fantasy*? It comes down to genre tropes. Every genre has its specific set of tropes that define it from others. Readers may not be able to name the tropes or be consciously aware of them; however, their subconscious mind will recognize them and determine whether they are ultimately satisfied or disappointed with the story.

When crafting an urban fantasy novel, it's notable to observe that the majority of novels are written in first-person past tense point-of-view. Readers browsing the top lists of urban fantasy books will likely find female protagonists dominating the charts, with male protagonists few and far between. For every Kate Daniels, Mercy Thompson, October Daye, and Anita Blake, there's one Harry Dresden.

The urban in urban fantasy usually refers to the setting, typically a bustling city. Again, for every rule you'll find a popular series that breaks it, such as Charlaine Harris' *Sookie Stackhouse* series or as many tv-watchers know them, the *True Blood* series.

In a typical urban fantasy novel, the smart and resourceful main character has to solve a problem, usually a murder or a hired job mission, with the help of allies along the way. Our snarky protagonist starts off as a loner type with one best

> Our snarky protagonist starts off as a loner type with one best friend but by the end of the book will have assembled a group of trusted friends, a found family.

friend but by the end of the book will have assembled a group of trusted friends, a found family.

Supernaturals can be hidden away or be living out in the open among humans. The distinction hasn't determined the success of urban fantasy books. Readers love both tropes, as long as there are plenty of interesting supernaturals in the mix. The usual supernaturals are witches and wizards, vampires, and shifters, but readers love the presence of fae, elves, and mythological creatures.

World-building is key. Showcase how the presence of supernaturals in the story elevates the mundane life to be mystical. Introduce several magical organizations that work behind-the-scenes to keep things under control. The protagonist could be a disillusioned employee of one of them and events cause them to branch out on their own.

Romance is not central to the storyline in urban fantasy books. Add too much of it and the book can lean toward paranormal romance. Some authors blend the two genres together, which could become a recipe for disaster. You may end up with a book that doesn't suit either target audience. The romantic subplot in urban fantasy usually unfolds over several books—a slow-burn romance. Love triangles were common years ago; however, recent trends lean toward a single romantic interest or in some cases, polyamorous relationships. The latter results with a female main character in love with several men, typically classified as reverse harem urban fantasy.

It's usual for urban fantasy books to be in a series rather than standalone novels. When fans of urban fantasy fall in love with a world and its misfit team of characters, they rarely want to

leave it. Each book should end with a promise for another mystery to be solved.

And last but not least, don't forget to add magic. Structure it so that the magic has rules; for every magical action there should be a reaction. It's dangerous to grant your protagonist unlimited power. Make them relatable with flaws, and be sure that the magic doesn't solve every problem they encounter. Keep it interesting and have it create problems for your protagonist.

All these elements combined can create a compelling world for readers to get lost in and result in a satisfactory experience. Stick to the tropes and add your own spin on them to keep them fresh. ■

Fatima Fayez

> When fans of urban fantasy fall in love with a world and its misfit team of characters, they rarely want to leave it.

Play
to
Win

Stack
the Odds
in Your Favor
with the Friday Five
from Indie Author Tools.
A free weekly email with the
best indie author tips, tools, and tech.

https://writelink.to/iat

# Connecting the Drops: Proper Hydration and Your Imagination

Does your creativity wane when you need it to wax? Are you staring at a blank page with no inspiration and a deadline? Do you feel frustrated, cranky, and tired? No need to despair—you have not been abandoned by your muse; you are probably just dehydrated!

Multiple studies have shown even mild dehydration results in fatigue, headaches, and irritability. Dehydration impairs function for tasks such as mental math, proofreading, and grammatical reasoning. This makes a lot of sense—the human brain is approximately 75% water. Proper hydration is essential for the brain to maintain optimal function. Benefits of optimal brain function include better mood, clearer thinking, and feeling more alert, just to name a few. Staying hydrated can boost your creativity and creative thinking.

How much water does one need to achieve optimal brain function? That depends on your size, weight, and activity level. According to multiple sources, you should drink half an ounce to an ounce of water for every pound of body weight each day. An active person in a hot climate or someone who exercises frequently would be on the higher end of this range. A person in a cooler climate or someone who is more sedentary would be in the lower range.

What is the best way to drink all this water? One sip at a time! Choose a new favorite cup, tumbler, or water bottle, and determine how many refills are needed to hit your daily hydration goal. If you struggle to meet your goal, try adding fruit slices, mint leaves, or a few drops of lemon or lime juice.

The next time you feel cranky, sluggish, or out of sorts, skip the afternoon iced coffee or cuppa, and fill up your water bottle instead. ■

Ashli Faron

> Staying hydrated can boost your creativity and creative thinking.

# CONQUERING THE MUDDY MIDDLE

**W**hen the shine of a new story idea fades and the muddy middle beckons, it is easy to lose interest, especially with a shaky or problematic plot. Giving up would be easy to do, so how do we keep going?

The actions in the middle often depend on the story's outcome. When the two cannot be connected in a linear fashion, take permission to jump ahead. Write exciting scenes from future chapters. This may connect the dots and give direction where so far there has been none. If that doesn't help, make note of points to remember and carry on to the denouement of the novel, returning at the end.

Another way is allowing characters room to breathe. Let them roam in temporary chapters. What would they do if they were just hanging out? Who would they meet and what would they say? New characteristics could be discovered, creating more depth and relatability, along with useful possibilities for the plot.

In contrast, introducing a new character, killing one, or being mean by exacerbating the protagonist's flaws to explore their dark side will escalate drama and conflict, especially if the world around them is shaken up too. Maybe it's time for a different character to have a turn in the spotlight.

Writing prompts in word sprints, or brainstorming with friends, using characters, settings, and vague story directions could bring insights on motivations, subplots impinging the protagonist, and other activities. Failing that, time away from the computer, completing mundane tasks or having a day without writing might refill the author well and allow new ideas to spring to mind or plot points tied in knots to unravel.

No matter what, refuse to quit over the muddy middle of despair, and remember why the novel was started in the first place. ◼

Anne Lown

**Refuse to quit over the muddy middle of despair.**

# The Many Faces of Author Collaboration

### WHAT IS COLLABORATION?

When two authors love each other very much… Okay, they don't have to love each other but the best collaborations do emerge from professional relationships based on trust, respect, and reliability.

Author collaboration has many faces. Whichever method of collaboration you are considering, the important thing to remember is that this is a business relationship. Anyone going into it should have frank discussions about what their expectations are. If you discover

half way through that your collaborator has conflicting expectations, it could wind up being a huge waste of time. Whichever way you plan to distribute the workload and publish the work, you need to be sure you have a contract.

Partnerships can be 50/50, 70/30, sliced-and-diced however the parties feel most comfortable.

Jon and James Evans (The Royal Marine Space Commandos series) are brothers. They meet to outline and plot, then write alternate chapters before editing each other's work. Jon explained, "We collaborate well, because we are not combative brothers—I don't think it would work well if you had a sibling you argue with all the time."

He continued that having two authors working on the same manuscript has its challenges. "Anything we use has to be good for two people working on a document in such a way there is never a conflict. Google Docs is good for that." Jon advises nailing down the tech and tools early. "It's worth working out where all your information, documents, and world-building stuff is going to be stored and how. I'd encourage anyone setting up a collaboration to go over all that."

Both parties writing is only one way to divide the work. There are other methods, such as one writes/one edits, or, one plots/one writes. A model which isn't considered often is when one person writes the books and the other markets them. In this scenario, thought must be given to the value of each partner's time. It might take six months to write the book but the marketing will be ongoing. What if the book doesn't sell? It's easy to come away from a collaboration feeling burned.

The best collaborations emerge from professional relationships based on trust, respect, and reliability.

Senior/junior relationships are popular with big name authors like James Patterson. They'll take on an upcoming author, giving them greater exposure, and enhancing their career. While they, themselves, have the opportunity to build their back catalog.

For the "senior partner" who is not interested in mentoring, a work-for-hire collaboration is another way to build a catalog quickly. In this collaboration, the one author pays another a fixed fee for writing a book. They assume the risk—if the book flops, the writer gets paid regardless—but also the rewards—all the royalties, should the book be a success. From the writer's perspective,

not every author wants to see their name in lights. They're not interested in waiting to earn royalties, because they've got bills to pay now. They want to write the book, get paid, and move on to the next project. An in-between approach could see the writer swap an equal share in royalties for an up-front payment and a reduced percentage of the royalties.

Round table collaboration is where a group of authors will get together and write in a shared universe. This model increases production and has been used to great success by Michael Anderle in his Kurtherian Gambit universe and Martha Carr in the Oriceran universe.

> "The most important thing with collaboration is to leave your ego at the door

Lucy Score, Claire Kingsley, Kathryn Nolan, and Pippa Grant did this for the Bluewater Billionaires series successfully as well. It ensures the fans always have something new to read based in their favorite fictional worlds. When Nicole Grotepas, author of the Holly Drake space opera series, had an idea for an urban fantasy story, she took the idea to Jamie Davis. There were similarities to his Extreme Medical Services urban fantasy series, and they decided to write the story together and set it in his EMS universe. They told us how they settled quickly into complementary roles in their collaboration for an anthology short story. Nicole had collaborated with another author previously and had experienced challenges around communication. For this collaboration, she and Jamie worked closely on the story beats and the outline over zoom calls. Jamie was keen that Nicole's voice be the dominant one in the story, so she wrote the first draft and sent it to him to weave it into his world. Jamie told us, "One of the key things about any collaboration is a key designation of who is responsible for what, and have a clear goal for what the outcome is."

On the subject of his collaboration with Brian Herbert and the continuing series of the Dune books, Kevin J. Anderson told us that "the most important thing with collaboration is to leave your ego at the door. This is a shared experience, like two people rowing a boat. Brian and I have written 3 million words together (and just this afternoon spent an hour on Zoom brainstorming the new Dune book, which wraps up a trilogy.) It's a delightful exchange of ideas, like a jazz performance, and together we produce something neither of us could do individually. But you HAVE TO compromise, roll with the changes, and produce the best work."

In his book *Collaborations,* Craig Martelle explains his belief that the whole is greater than the sum of its parts. That two people working together can create a piece of work that neither might have been capable of alone. Craig has collaborated many times for many of the reasons suggested above. He believes it can be rewarding with the right person—someone you trust, someone with the same goals and expectations as you. As he is known to say, "Under-promise and over deliver" for a positive outcome.

## CONTRACTS

When and if you have to walk away, that's where the importance of having a contract comes in. Write a solid contract that will allow the parties to walk away and remain friends. Jamie and Nicole are working on a contract for their short story. Even Jon and James Evans' work with each other is covered by a contract and with anyone else they work with.

The contract should include workload, who does what. Deliverables, make them SMART. Ensure you know who pays for what. Whose name is on the cover first, how and when parties will receive royalties. A contract isn't just for the parties working together, but for their heirs. You don't want to leave your grandkids at each other's throats. Make sure the contract is clear about how to handle both failure (who pays for the production costs and how is the time already

> Work with someone you trust, behave ethically, roll up your sleeves, and get to work.

spent compensated?) and incredible success (how are royalties divided if Netflix comes calling?).

Ultimately, you have to decide if the benefits to collaboration outweigh the risks. If this is a direction you're considering, speak to people with experience, learn the pitfalls, read books like Craig Martelle's *Collaborations*, making sure you check out the sample contracts in the back of the book. Get a lawyer, work with someone you trust, behave ethically, roll up your sleeves, and get to work. ▪

Elaine Bateman

# Books We Love

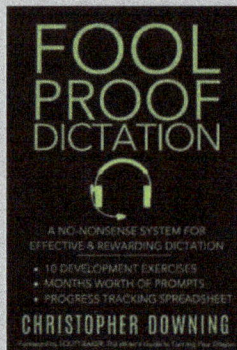

Do you use talk to text to send emails? Why not utilize the same technology capable of keeping up with your writing? This book focuses primarily on the mental process of dictation. It's a self-paced training system that streamlines the dictation process. There are warm-ups, practical exercises, and an easy to follow routine for dictating your scenes.

indieauthortools.com/
fool-proof-dictation

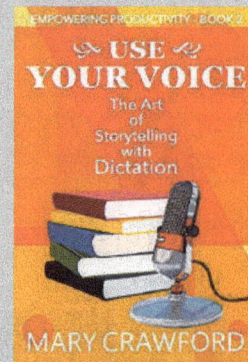

This book helps you with the fundamentals of using dictation to write your stories. It also provides an overview of popular writing software and how those programs interact with dictation software. Learn about what is standard in the industry and empower yourself to choose the software and equipment that will best meet your needs.

indieauthortools.com/
use-your-voice-the-art-of-sto-
rytelling-with-dictation-em-
powering-productivity-book-2

This book provides a great introduction to the world of dictation software. It also provides an indepth look at the latest releases from Nuance, including Dragon® Professional Individual for Mac 6.0.8 (Dragon® Dictate) and Dragon® Professional Individual 15.3 for Windows (Dragon® NaturallySpeaking), and discusses how they stack up against other alternatives.

indieauthortools.com/
the-power-of-dictation-empowering-productivity-book-1

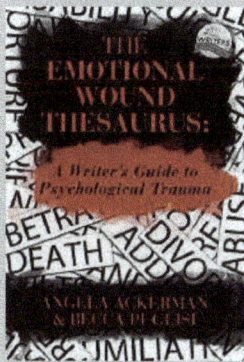

Root your characters in reality by giving them an authentic wound that causes difficulties and prompts them to strive for inner growth to overcome it. With its easy-to-read format and over 100 entries packed with information, The Emotional Wound Thesaurus is a crash course in psychology for creating characters that feel incredibly real to readers.

indieauthortools.com/the-emotional-wound-the-saurus-a-writers-guide-to-psychological-trauma-2

Don't stop telling your story to explain what is happening to a character. Elevate your writing by minimizing exposition. In Show, Don't Tell, you'll learn how to write descriptions, backstory, and emotions in a way that is captivating to readers and ensuring the pacing of your plot doesn't suffer.

indieauthortools.com/show-dont-tell

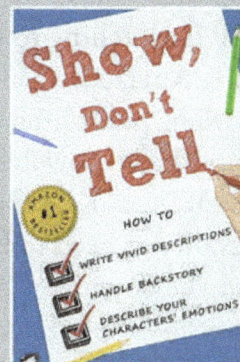

# INDIE AUTHOR NEWS

### ADS FOR AUTHORS

Ads for Authors from Mark Dawson's Self Publishing Formula (SPF) launches again on 9th June and will stay open for around 2-3 weeks. The course will be available to buy with a single outright payment of $849, or can be split across twelve or even twenty-four months ($75 or $45 a month, respectively.) To join the waitlist and be notified when the course opens again, sign up at https://selfpublishingformula.com/ads-waitlist.

### REMINDER
### KDP TO BE EPUB ONLY

Amazon KDP is switching to EPUB only. After June 28, 2021, Amazon will no longer support MOBI files when publishing new or updating previously published reflowable eBooks. Instead, use EPUB, DOCX, or KPF formats for uploads. Existing titles do not need to be changed unless you re-upload the document.

https://writelink.to/r6ir8x

### THE COVER DESIGNER DIRECTORY

The Cover Designer Directory was recently launched. It provides a curated selection of high-quality, indie-minded, talented, and ethical cover designers.

https://writelink.to/38n2fl

### CLUBHOUSE FOR ANDROID

Clubhouse for Android is now available in the US, and available for pre-registration elsewhere (and slowly rolling out.) Want to know more about this new social platform? Check out 10 Tips for Clubhouse.

### IAM OPINIONATED

Social Media for authors:
Way to Connect or Waste of Time?

Have your say!
Vote here
https://writelink.to/
iamopinionated

# INDIE AUTHOR EVENTS

For the latest on news and events pertinent to the Indie Author community, please check out our interactive calendar here:

Got news or events to share with the Indie Author Community? Let us know at news@indieauthormagazine.com.

# In This Issue

## Executive Team

### Chelle Honiker, Publisher

As the publisher of Indie Author Magazine, Chelle Honiker brings nearly three decades of startup, technology, training, and executive leadership experience to the role. She's a serial entrepreneur, founding and selling multiple successful companies including a training development company, travel agency, website design and hosting firm, a digital marketing consultancy, and a wedding planning firm. She's organized and curated multiple TEDx events and hired to assist other nonprofit organizations as a fractional executive, including The Travel Institute and The Freelance Association.

As a writer, speaker, and trainer she believes in the power of words and their ability to heal, inspire, incite, and motivate. Her greatest inspiration is her daughters, Kelsea and Cathryn, who tolerate her tendency to run away from home to play with her friends around the world for months at a time. It's said she could run a small country with just the contents of her backpack.

### Alice Briggs, Creative Director

As the creative director of Indie Author Magazine, Alice Briggs utilizes her more than three decades of artistic exploration and expression, business startup adventures, and leadership skills. A serial entrepreneur, she has started several successful businesses. She brings her experience in creative direction, magazine layout and design, and graphic design in and outside of the indie author community to her role.

With a masters of science in Occupational Therapy, she has a broad skill set and uses it to assist others in achieving their desired goals. As a writer, teacher, healer, and artist, she loves to see people accomplish all they desire. She's excited to see how IAM will encourage many authors to succeed in whatever way they choose. She hopes to meet many of you in various places around the world once her passport is back in use.

### Erika Everest, Managing Editor

Over fifteen years in the corporate sector, managing international projects and teams, gives Erika Everest a strong foundation for managing the globally-dispersed editorial team working at Indie Author Magazine.

She has co-curated eight anthologies in the past three years, and works with authors for proofreading, beta reading, editing, formatting, and newsletter set up and maintenance.

With a PhD in Biostatistics and a postgraduate qualification in International Business Management, Erika values strategic and analytical thinking. She also values unicorns, tiaras, and happily ever afters. She has published three novels in a series of fairytale retellings, and likes to procrastinate by writing nonfiction books to help authors.

## Robyn Sarty, Managing Editor

As a managing editor at Indie Author Magazine, Robyn Sarty brings over a decade of experience as an editor and proofreader. She is the author of two novels and several short stories, and manages her own publishing company. She loves helping other authors with their books and can often be found nerding out over story elements with her friends. She spent five years as a project coordinator for an international engineering firm, and now uses those skills to chase writers instead of engineers and hopes it will be good training for her first marathon.

Growing up as a third culture kid, books were the one constant in her life, and as such, Robyn believes that books are portals to the magic that lies within, and authors are wielders of that magic. She also admits to being a staunch, loyal, and unabashed supporter of the Oxford comma.

## Staff Writers

### Elaine Bateman

In her pre-author life, Elaine worked for FTSE 100 and Fortune 500 companies in procurement, project support, and IT Training. She has a bachelor of scienceBSc. in Systems Practice and Design.

She is the author of eight published fiction novels and is working on her ninth.

Elaine enjoys giving back to the writing community through her work with 20Booksto50k, an online author community.

She was the Acorn Sports Bar Ladies' Yard-of-Ale Speed-drinking champion of 1985 (she was the only lady to enter and it took her all night.)

She lives in the UK with her husband, son, and three dogs. She no longer drinks ale.

### Laurel Decher

There might be no frigate like a book, but publishing can feel like a voyage on the H.M.S. Surprise. There's always a twist and there's never a moment to lose.

Laurel's mission is to help you make the most of today's opportunities. She's a strategic problem-solver, tool collector, and co-inventor of the "you never know" theory of publishing.

As an epidemiologist, she studied factors that help babies and toddlers thrive. Now she writes books for children ages nine to twelve about finding more magic in life. She's a member of the Society for Children's Book Writers and Illustrators (SCBWI), has various advanced degrees, and a tendency to smuggle vegetables into storylines.

### Marion Hermannsen

Marion is a bilingual author, working in both German and English. She holds a masters of artsan MA in English, Spanish, and Italian, as well as a DipM (Marketing). She spent thirteen years both in London and Ireland while working in the finance and consulting industry.

Marion loves learning about writing craft and marketing best practices. She spends time mentoring other writers and enjoys the freedom of being able to work from anywhere.

She now lives in Frankfurt and is an active member of the local writing community, having published eight novels to date.

Her Irish husband has not only taught her the benefits of drinking copious amounts of black tea, but has impressed his Irish accent on her, to the amusement of her friends and colleagues.

## Chrishaun Keller-Hanna

Chrishaun Keller-Hanna is an award-winning journalist, teacher, technical writer, and fiction author that lives for explaining difficult concepts in a way that non-technical readers can understand.

She spent twenty years teaching literacy and composition to a variety of students from kindergarten to college level and writing technical documentation for several tech companies in the Austin area. At the age of forty-three, she decided to write fiction and has published over thirty titles so far with plans to extend out to comics and board games.

When she's not writing, she's traveling, playing video games, or watching movies. When she's not doing THAT, she's talking about them with her husband and grown daughters.

## Anne Lown

Postal worker-turned-author, Anne Lown's career in the postal service, and her previous life in picturesque Devon, inevitably led to an interest in the small-town element of cozy mysteries. As she sorted the mail, she considered how evil can lurk behind the most delightful of settings.

Thankfully, she became an author, not a serial killer.

Anne has had the privilege of moderating the Facebook group for authors, 20Booksto50K, since 2018 and has delighted in cheering on fellow authors as their careers have grown and blossomed. She also runs the YouTube channel for the group.

Anne is the author of four novels and is working on the next in the current series, with others in development. At home, she is a life-long learner and hoarder of courses, much to the horror of her son. Her dog's interests are food and sleep.

## Sìne Màiri MacDougall

Sìne Màiri is a Gàidhlig speaker from the Nova Scotian Gaidhealtachd. She's an author, international incident starter, and recovering educator. Having taught all over the world from the UK to Northern Canada to China, and back again, her specialties are language and literature, history, and youth services for alternative education. She unapologetically writes about the themes she's encountered in her travels; resilience and found family being chief amongst those themes.

Her current fiction projects include two urban fantasy series that she hopes to launch in the coming year.

## Susan Odev

Susan has banked over three decades of work experience in the fields of personal and organizational development, being a freelance corporate trainer and consultant alongside holding down "real" jobs for over twenty-five years. Specializing in entrepreneurial mindsets, she has written several non-fiction business books, once gaining a coveted Amazon #1 best seller tag in business and entrepreneurship, an accolade she now strives to emulate with her fiction.

Currently working on her fifth novel, under a top secret pen name, the craft and marketing aspects of being a successful indie author equally fascinate and terrify her.

A lover of history with a criminal record collection, Susan lives in a retro orange and avocado world. Once described by a colleague as being an "onion," Susan has many layers, as have ogres (according to Shrek). She would like to think this makes her cool, her teenage children just think she's embarrassing.

## Contributors

### Fatima Fayez

As a contributing writer for Indie Author Magazine, Fatima unites her love of connecting with people and giving back to the author community. She is a co-founder of The Author Arena podcast, in addition to The Author Conference on Clubhouse. She is also an administrator for the 20BooksTo50K® Facebook group.

Fatima has lived in countries across Europe, Asia, and North America. During her various residencies, she managed to collect a bachelor of science in Journalism, along with a masters in Business Administration, and a handful of management certifications. She currently resides in Kuwait with her family.

On Saturdays, you can find her playing Dungeons & Dragons with her party.

### Kasia Lasinska

Kasia Lasinska holds an LLB in Law with European Legal Studies and an LL.M. in Advanced Studies in International Law. As a practicing attorney, Kasia worked with a top international human rights barrister and then advised clients at a large, international law firm. These inspired her to write dystopian and fantasy novels about corrupt governments and teenagers saving the world.

Kasia lived in eight countries and speaks five languages (fluently after a glass of wine). She currently lives in London, but her daydreams are filled with beaches and palm trees.

When she's not writing, you can find Kasia scouting out the best coffee shops in town, planning her next great adventure, or petting other people's puppies.

### Kevin McLaughlin

Kevin McLaughlin is the USA Today bestselling author of 83 books. He writes mostly science fiction and fantasy, and is also the author of The Coffee Break Novelist and You Must Write. He's enjoyed reading and writing serials for decades.

# Don't Gamble with Your Author Career...

Go all in at the biggest indie author conference
November 8-12, 2021 Las Vegas, NV, USA

**200+ presentations:** Something for everyone at every point in your publishing journey

**Industry day:** Meet the distributors, service providers, and more!

**Author signing day:** Be a vendor, meet your favorite authors, and/or see how it's done by some of the best.

**Plus:** Many networking opportunities during the conference and after hours. Meet others in your genre or who share a special interest.

**20 BOOKS TO 50K®**

Join the 20Booksto50K® Facebook group for more info!

https://writelink.to/20Books

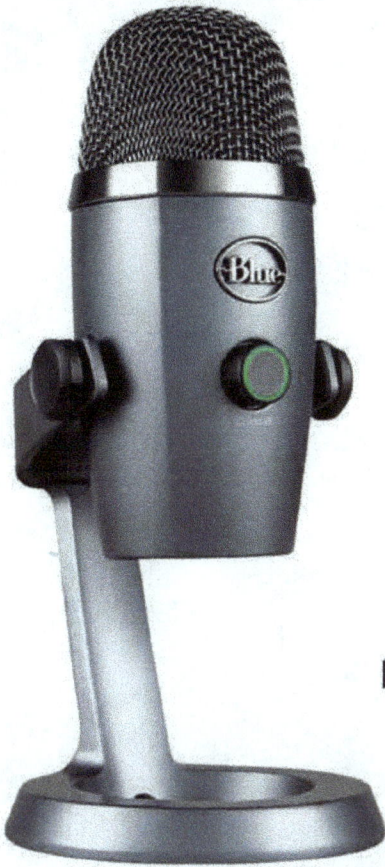

9781948666299